NOT YOUR GRANNY'S GRANNY SQUARES

for Babies and Kids

Babette Ulmer

NOT YOUR GRANNY'S GRANNY SQUARES

for Babies and Kids

Crochet Adorable Clothes,
Toys, and More!

weldonowen

CONTENTS

INTRODUCTION

I'm delighted to introduce you to my new book, which once again focuses on the wonderful world of granny squares—with enchanting designs for babies and toddlers. Whether for your own child, for your grandchildren, or as a thoughtful gift, these projects made from granny squares are not only practical but also real eye-catchers.

For me, crocheting is more than just a technique—it's a way to create something beautiful with my hands, experiencing moments of peace and contentment. And I want to convey precisely this joy to you with my new designs. You'll find a colorful variety of projects that are as diverse as the little ones they're intended for: cozy blankets, cute toys, adorable garments, and much more.

The instructions for each project are simple and easy to understand, so even beginners can quickly achieve brilliant results. Each granny square is a small work of art in its own right, made unique by your personal color choice and your own ideas. Be inspired, experiment different colors and shapes, and above all: Enjoy the creative process!

I invite you to create these designs with your hands—and with plenty of heart. Experience how a simple granny square can become a magical companion for our little ones, and embrace the joy and love conveyed by crocheting.

I hope you enjoy reading this book and recreating the designs, and I wish you every success.

With warm regards and best wishes for your creative endeavors,

Babette Ulmer

GRANNY SQUARES: THE BASICS

GRANNY SQUARES

Granny squares are adorable small crochet squares that you can seam up patchwork style to create all sorts of beautiful things. No matter whether you work them in a fabulous mix of bright colors or in monochrome, no matter whether they look cheerful, elegant, or wildly exciting—they are eye-catching throughout the seasons, zhuzh up any outfit as a small and stylish detail, or act as a building block for an allover pattern.

WHO INVENTED THEM?

Mrs Phelps. A short answer to a question that no one answered for a long time. In a publication, American home economics TV icon Martha Stewart claimed that European settlers had crocheted granny squares in their covered wagons as early as in the 17th century. Male and female historians disagreed with her statement: crochet had been unknown at that time, and pioneer women only knew how to weave and, at best, knit. Authors of German needlecraft books speculated that granny squares were a post-war invention—equally wrong as there is plenty of evidence of older granny square patterns.

Those interested in both crochet and history have browsed historical needlecraft books, looking for the first instructions for the crochet square that was to become such a global success. The oldest known find so far is a book called *Art of Crocheting* (1891) with an illustration of a crochet square that bears an uncanny resemblance to today's modern classic. However, only clusters of two double crochets were worked, instead of clusters of three, as is mainly the case nowadays.

In February 2022, Ruth and Joy, a mother-and-daughter team from New Zealand who run The Yarn Queen, a wool shop, announced exciting news in their blog: The crochet square pattern didn't appear in a needlework book for the very first time but in an agricultural magazine! On April 4, 1885, the *Prairie Farmer Magazine* reported about a meeting of the Housewives Club, during which a certain Mrs Phelps (no first name given) introduced a new crochet pattern—a perfect granny square with three double crochet clusters, color changes in each round, and multicolored tones in the center and a black edging.

It was supposed to be the basis for a crochet blanket, and Mrs. Phelps called it "pattern for a

crazy afghan" (the latter was a term for a wool blanket in the 19th century). The word "crazy" referred to a modern quilting technique that involved assembling brightly colored patchwork squares with black velvet ribbon. Thus, the year 1885 was the beginning of the granny square's success story.

Granny squares became popular globally in the last 138 years. No wonder, as they are easy to crochet and can be worked whenever and wherever you want. They are perfect for using up leftover yarns and experimenting with colors, and you can assemble the squares for a plethora of projects—from blankets to tops, jackets, and sweaters in all possible sizes. Over the years, the crochet square's name changed to granny square. Why that happened isn't quite clear, and speculations abound. The simple pattern can be crocheted with failing eyesight or even when blind—hence the connection to the older generation. Grandmothers seem to have the time and leisure to sew the individual squares together, so the finished piece of work was credited to them. Another idea for the name change might be that these striking crochet patterns have been on trend for so long that everyone knows them from their grandmothers!

All that aside, a big thank you to Mrs. Phelps! She clearly inspired the world of crochet and made this craft a lot more vibrant, even when her crazy afghan pattern turned into a granny square.

BABIES AND KIDS

Granny squares have been an integral part of the crochet world for more than 100 years and offer countless design possibilities, even for baby and children's clothes. These adorable small squares made of crochet stitches make perfect projects for beginners, yet offer those more advanced in the art of crochet the opportunity to create imaginative and individual children's clothing.

The magic of granny squares is their versatility. These small squares can be made from a variety of colors and yarns, allowing you to create clothing and accessories in any style you like. Whether vibrant and colorful for a cheerful children's outfit or delicate pastel shades for baby clothes, the choice of color combinations is endless, making every project unique.

Unaffected by fashion and the spirit of the times, granny square baby blankets have been around for many generations, and are pretty much known by all. Used as swaddling blankets, for strollers or as crawling mats, they're cozy and easy to care for, lightweight, quick to pack for travel, and a truly cheerful eye-catcher in any size. You can easily enlarge a granny square blanket by simply adding more squares, or using less squares for a smaller blanket.

Granny squares can be used for rompers or baby jackets. Combine them in a stunning color gradient or as a combination of harmonious shades, keeping the design fresh and interesting.

Whether it's children's clothing, or hats, scarves, and even small bags made from granny squares, my new projects are both functional and cute, adding a subtle or bold touch depending on your color choice. The ease and comfort of these garments simply make them ideal for everyday use.

Granny squares are quick to crochet and can be worked individually in stages. This is especially useful if you're tackling a larger project as you can work on the squares one at a time and even on the go. Assembling the squares is fun as you can see straight away how the individual pieces come together to create a work of art.

SMALL, COLORFUL, MODULAR

• In general, granny squares are small and square, approximately 2 in x 2 in to 6 in x 6 in in size, but you can change the size as you wish.

• Traditionally, granny squares are made from many different colors that you can combine any way you like. You often see the characteristic combination of bold, contrasting colors that gives the pattern its distinctive appeal.

• You often begin granny squares with a foundation ring or magic loop, crochet around it in rounds, and close it by firmly tightening the yarn tail; it creates an optical center that later appears as an almost floral design.

• Granny squares are worked individually and, when finished, sewn or crocheted together to make larger projects, such as blankets, cushions, bag, jackets, or scarves.

YARNS

When it comes to crocheting baby and children's clothes, choose your yarn carefully. After all, the delicate skin of our little ones has special needs that can be optimally met and supported by choosing the correct material. Bear in mind the following qualities of yarn when crocheting for babies and children:

Cotton is a classic for baby and children's clothing. It's skin-friendly, breathable, and soft—ideal for sensitive skin. Cotton is also a robust, natural material that is easy to wash and retains its shape even after frequent washing. It's a particularly good choice for summer garments, such as rompers, hats, or small blankets. If you're looking for really soft and fine cotton, go for Peruvian pima or Egyptian cotton, both known for their softness and high quality.

Merino wool is an excellent choice for garments worn in the colder months of the year. Apart from its moisture-regulating properties, it's exceptionally soft and doesn't scratch the skin. Merino wool is perfect for baby jackets, hats, or blankets, because it keeps children warm without adding bulk. Make sure to choose merino wool from certified, responsibly managed sources to be kind both to skin and the environment. Depending on the project, it's worth choosing a yarn that is easy to wash.

Bamboo yarn is becoming increasingly popular, mainly due to its environmentally friendly properties and remarkable softness. It's naturally hypoallergenic and ideal for babies with sensitive skin or suffering from skin problems like eczema. In addition, bamboo yarn has a cooling effect, making it suitable for warmer climates or as a summer yarn. It gives clothes a beautiful luster and silky feel.

Alpaca is a luxurious, hypoallergenic fiber know for its exceptional softness and warmth. It doesn't scratch, making it ideal for baby and children's clothing that comes into direct contact with skin. Alpaca wool has thermo-regulating properties, keeping you warm without overheating. Make sure to choose well-made alpaca yarn, as it's not always as durable as merino wool or cotton in its natural state.

Although natural yarns are always preferred, **high-quality acrylic yarn** is a practical and cost-effective alternative for baby and children's accessories. It's particularly easy to care for because acrylic is machine washable and retains its shape and color even after frequent washing. Furthermore, acrylic yarns are often available in a wide range of colors and weights. For small items like toys or blankets, acrylic can be a good choice as it's robust and durable.

Another interesting option for baby and children's clothes are **yarn blends**. Cotton and acrylic blends are skin friendly and durable; whereas wool and cotton blends combine the advantages of both materials: the softness and warmth of wool and the breathability of cotton. These blends are often less expensive and easier to care for than pure natural fibers.

YARNS AND SIZES, TIPS AND TRICKS

In principle, you can use all yarns for granny squares, but of course they look different when worked with various yarns. When you crochet a granny square with the same number of rounds but a thinner yarn and a smaller crochet hook, it'll be smaller; using a coarser yarn and a thicker hook will turn the granny square into a larger one.

Depending on the choice of the material and the size of the crochet hook, the granny square can become firm and stiff, or loose and airy. Granny squares made from cotton yarns tend to appear stiffer when finished, contrary to wool and fantasy yarns. For clothing, it is better to crochet loosely so that the sweater or the jacket falls nicely. On the other hand, for home decor accessories you may prefer a slightly firmer piece of crochet work.

SIZE AND SHAPE

You can vary the size of a granny square in different ways. Simply crocheting more rounds is one possibility, but it may result in the top or sweater being too wide or too tight, as the increase or decrease adds up several times when lining up the squares next to each other.

To adjust this more finely, you could add "smaller" rounds of single crochets around the square at the end. This is important, for example, when using a different yarn than the one for the original project.

You can also work a granny square in another geometric shape. In this book I use triangles and rectangles as well to create all cuts and shapes.

SEWING OR CROCHETING TOGETHER

I have crocheted together most of the granny squares used for the projects in this book with slip stitches. Alternatively, you can sew them together working overlock stitches that give you a flat, almost invisible seam. Of course, there are other ways of sewing or crocheting together the individual squares and parts. For example, to give the sides of the Animal Block (pp 108–111) more stability, the parts were crocheted together with 1 row single crochets.

TIPS AND TRICKS

For a neat transition from one round to the next, I didn't use the usual slip stitch but a half double crochet. That way, you won't need further slip stitches to get to the actual starting point of the round.

To avoid having to fasten off the thread ends, or tails, you can "hide" them while crocheting. Simply place the tail (or tails) parallel to your crochet work, and work the stitches not only around the square (or any other shape) but also around the tails.

For a nice color transition with multicolored granny squares, always work the last stitch before the color change in the new color.

GRANNY SQUARE

INSTRUCTIONS

Round 1: Around an adjustable foundation ring (= magic loop) crochet 3 turning chains, 2 double crochets, 3x (2 chain stitches, 3 double crochets), 1 half double crochet in the 3rd turning chain. Tighten the foundation ring.

Round 2: (3 turning chains, 2 double crochets) in the half double crochet of the lower round, 3x [(3 double crochets, 3 chains, 3 double crochets) around the chain space of the round below], 3 double crochets in the half double crochet of the round below, 1 half double crochet in the 3rd turning chain.

Round 3: (3 turning chains, 2 double crochets) in the half double crochet of the round below, 3x [3 double crochets in the gap between 2 double crochet clusters, (3 double crochets, 3 chains, 3 double crochets) around the chain space of the round below], 3 double crochets in the gap between 2 double crochet clusters, 3 double crochets in the half double crochet of the round below, 1 half double crochets in the 3rd turning chain.

Round 4: (3 turning chains, 2 double crochets) in the half double crochet of the round below, 2x (3 double crochets in the gap between 2 double crochet clusters), 3x [(3 double crochets, 3 chains, 3 double crochets) around the chain space of the round below, 2x (3 double crochets in the gap between 2 double crochet clusters)], 3 double crochets in the half double crochets of the round below, 1 half double crochet in the 3rd turning chain.

Round 5: (3 turning chains, 2 double crochets) in the half double crochet of the round below, 3x (3 double crochets in the gap between 2 double crochet clusters), 3x [(3 double crochets, 3 chains, 3 double crochets) around the chain space of the round below, 3x (3 double crochets in the gap between 2 double crochet clusters)], 3 double crochets in the half double crochet of the round below, close the round with 3 chains and 1 slip stitch in the 3rd turning chain.

Note: According to the same principle, you can enlarge the granny square with each further round by crocheting 1 double crochet cluster more per side in between the double crochet clusters of the round below. Close the last round as described in Round 5.

TIP For a neat transition change the color before decreasing the half double crochet at the end of the round.

Crochet diagram

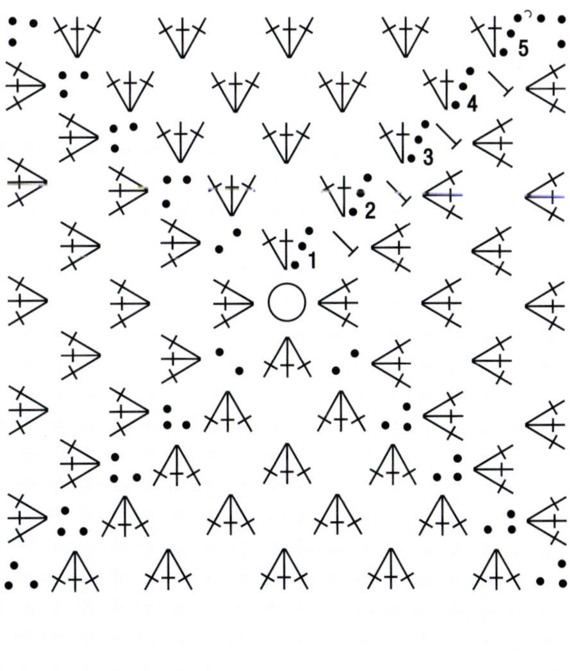

Key

- • = 1 chain stitch
- c = 1 slip stitch
- T = 1 half double crochet
- † = 1 double crochet

If the symbols meet at the bottom, insert the hook into the same stitch.

GRANNY TRIANGLE

INSTRUCTIONS

Row 1: Around an adjustable foundation ring (= magic loop) crochet 4 chain stitches, 3 double crochets, 2 chains, 3 double crochets, 1 chain, 1 double crochet. Tighten the foundation ring.
Row 2: 4 turning chains in the double crochet of the lower row, 3 double crochets around the following chains, (3 double crochets, 3 chains, 3 double crochets) around the chain space of the row, below (3 double crochets, 1 chain, 1 double crochet) around the turning chains of the row below.
Row 3: 4 turning chains in the double crochet of the row below, 3 double crochets around the following chains, 3 double crochets in the gap between 2 double crochet clusters, (3 double crochets, 3 chains, 3 double crochets) around the chain space of the row below, 3 double crochets in the gap between 2 double crochet clusters, (3 double crochets, 1 chain, 1 double crochet) around the turning chains of the row below.
Row 4: 4 turning chains in the double crochet of the row below, 3 double crochets around the following chains, 2x (3 double crochets in the gap between 2 double crochet clusters), (3 double crochets, 3 chains, 3 double crochets) around the chain space of the row below, 2x (3 double crochets in the gap between 2 double crochet clusters), (3 double crochets, 1 chain, 1 double crochet) around the turning chains of the row below.
Row 5: 4 turning chains in the double crochet of the row below, 3 double crochets around the following chains, 3x (3 double crochets in the gap between 2 double crochet clusters), (3 double crochets, 3 chains, 3 double crochets) around the chain space of the row below, 3x (3 double crochets in the gap between 2 double crochet clusters), (3 double crochets, 1 chain, 1 double crochet) around the turning chains of the row below.

Note: According to the same principle, you can enlarge the granny triangle as you wish by crocheting 1 double crochet cluster per side more in each further row between the double crochet clusters of the row below.

Crochet diagram

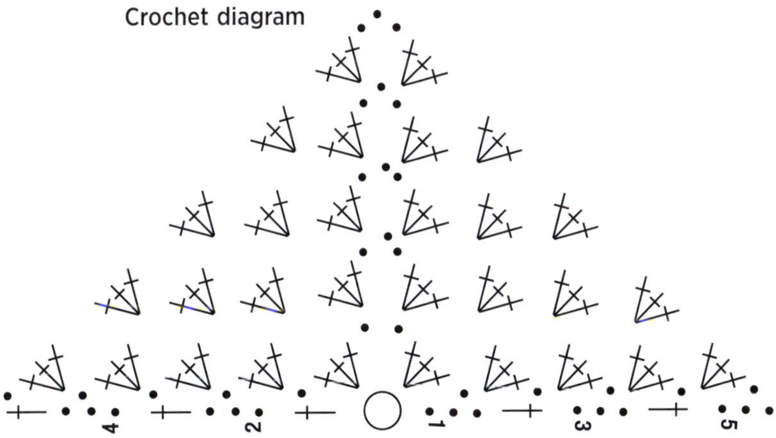

Key

- = 1 chain stitch

† = 1 double crochet

If the symbols meet at the bottom, insert the hook into the same stitch.

GRANNY RECTANGLE

INSTRUCTIONS

Row 1: Around an adjustable foundation ring (= magic loop) crochet 3 chain stitches, 1 double crochet, 2 chains, 3 double crochets, 2 chains, 2 double crochets. Tighten the foundation ring.

Row 2: 3 turning chains, 2x [(3 double crochets, 3 chains, 3 double crochets) around the chain space of the row below], 1 double crochet in the 3rd turning chain of the row below.

Row 3: (3 turning chains, 1 double crochet) in the double crochet of the row below, (3 double crochets, 3 chains, 3 double crochets) around the chain space of the row below, 3 double crochets in the gap between 2 double crochet clusters, (3 double crochets, 3 chains, 3 double crochets) around the chain space of the row below, 2 double crochets in the 3rd turning chain of the row below.

Row 4: 3 turning chains, 2x [3 double crochets in the gap between 2 double crochet clusters, (3 double crochets, 3 chains, 3 double crochets) around the chain space of the row below, 3 double crochets in the gap between 2 double crochet clusters], 1 double crochet in the 3rd turning chain of the row below.

Row 5: (3 turning chains, 1 double crochet) in the double crochet of the row below, 3 double crochets in the gap between 2 double crochet clusters, (3 double crochets, 3 chains, 3 double crochets) around the chain space of the row below, 3x [3 double crochets in the gap between 2 double crochet clusters], (3 double crochets, 3 chains, 3 double crochets) around the chain space of the row below, 3 double crochets in the gap between 2 double crochet clusters, 2 double crochets in the 3rd turning chain of the row below.

Note: According to the same principle, you can enlarge the granny rectangle as you wish by crocheting 1 double crochet cluster per side more in each further row between the double crochet clusters of the row below.

Crochet diagram

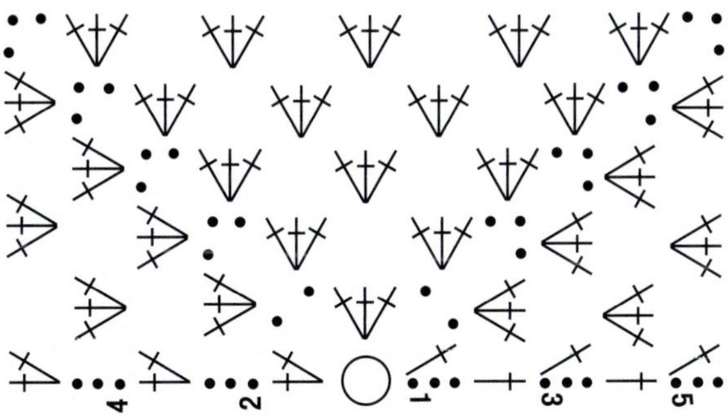

Key

• = 1 cain stitch

† = 1 double crochet

If the symbols meet at the bottom, insert the hook into the same stitch.

GRANNY FLOWER

INSTRUCTIONS

Round 1: Around an adjustable foundation ring (= magic loop) crochet 3 turning chains and 11 double crochets, close the round with 1 slip stitch in the topmost turning chain. Tighten the foundation ring.

Round 2: (3 turning chains, 2 double crochets together) in the 3rd turning chain of the row below, 2 chain stitches, 11x [3 double crochets together, 2 chains], close the round with 1 slip stitch in the topmost turning chain.

Round 3: 2 turning chains, * 3 half double crochets around the next chain space, (3 double crochets, 3 chains, 3 double crochets) around the next chain space, 3 half double crochets around the next chain space, work 3x from *, 3 half double crochets around the next chain space, (3 double crochets, 3 chains, 3 double crochets) around the next chain space, 2 half double crochets around the next chain space, close the round with 1 slip stitch in the topmost turning chain.

Round 4: (3 turning chains, 2 double crochets together) in the 3rd turning chain of the row below, * 3 double crochets around the next chain space, (3 double crochets, 3 chains, 3 double crochets) around the next chain space, 2x (3 double crochets) around the next chain space, work 3x from *, 3 double crochets around the next chain space, (3 double crochets, 3 chains, 3 double crochets) around the next chain space, 3 double crochets around the next chain space.

For a neat transition change the color before the slip stitch at the end of the round.

Note: You may enlarge the granny flower after these 4 rounds by crocheting further rounds as per Round 4. With each round add 1 double crochet cluster per side. To illustrate the principle, Round 5 has also been drawn in the crochet diagram; however, it isn't necessary for every project.

Round 5: (3 turning chains, 2 double crochets) in the 3rd turning chain of the round below, * 2x [3 double crochets around the next chain space], (3 double crochets, 3 chains, 3 double crochets) around the next chain space, 2x [3 double crochets around the next chain space], work 3x from *, 2x [3 double crochets around the next chain space], (3 double crochets, 3 chains, 3 double crochets) around the next chain space, 3 double crochets around the next chain space, close the round with 1 slip stitch into the topmost turning chain.

Crochet diagram

Key

- • = 1 chain stitch
- c = 1 slip stitch
- T = 1 half double crochet
- † = 1 double crochet
- = 2 double crochets together
- = 3 double crochets together

If the symbols meet at the bottom, insert the hook into the same stitch. If the symbols meet at the top, decrease the stitches together.

GRANNY CIRCLE

INSTRUCTIONS

Round 1: Around an adjustable foundation ring (= magic loop) crochet turning chains and 11 double crochets, close the round with 1 slip stitch in the topmost turning chain. Tighten the foundation chain.

Round 2: (3 turning chains, 1 double crochet) in the 3rd turning chain of the round below, 11x [2 double crochets in 1 stitch], close the round with 1 slip stitch in the topmost turning chain.

Round 3: 3 turning chains, 2 double crochets in 1 stitch, 11x [1 double crochet, 2 double crochets in 1 stitch], close the round with 1 slip stitch in the topmost turning chain.

Round 4: (3 turning chains, 1 double crochet) in the 3rd turning chain of the round below, 2 double crochets, 11x [2 double crochets in 1 stitch, 2 double crochets], close the round with 1 slip stitch in the topmost turning chain.

Round 5: (1 turning chain, 1 single crochet) in the 3rd turning chain of the round below, * 3 single crochets, 2 half double crochets, 1 double crochet, (1 double crochet, 2 treble crochets) in 1 stitch, 2 chain stitches, (2 treble crochets, 1 double crochet) in 1 stitch, 1 double crochet, 2 half double crochets, 1 single crochet, work 3x from *, 3 single crochets, 2 half double crochets, 1 double crochet, (1 double crochet, 2 treble crochets) in 1 stitch, 2 chains, (2 treble crochets, 1 double crochet) in 1 stitch, 1 double crochet, 2 half double crochets, close the round with 1 slip stitch in the topmost turning chain.

Round 6: 3 turning chains, 9 double crochets, * (2 double crochets, 2 chains, 2 double crochets) around the chain space, 16 double crochets, work 3x from *, (2 double crochets, 2 chains, 2 double crochets) around the chain space, 6 double crochets, close the round with 1 slip stitch in the topmost turning chain.

TIP For a neat transition change the color before the slip stitch at the end of the round.

Note: A smaller variation of this granny square over only 5 rounds for the animal faces is shown on p 108. A special crochet diagram is used there.

Crochet diagram

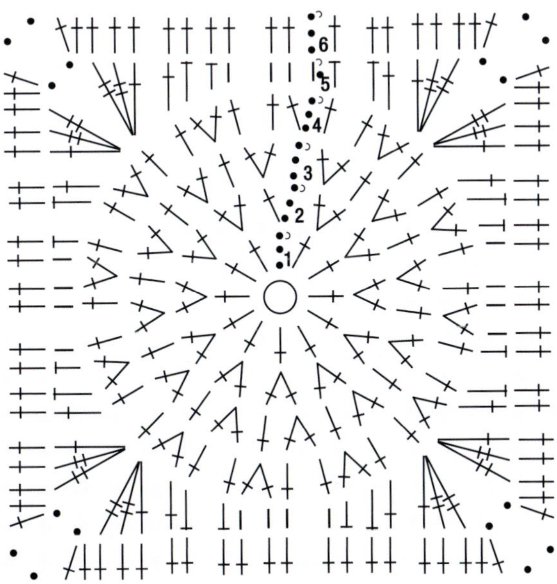

Key

• = 1 chain stitch

c = 1 slip stitch

| = 1 single crochet

T = 1 half double crochet

† = 1 double crochet

‡ = 1 treble crochet

If the symbols meet at the bottom, insert the hook into the same stitch. If the symbols meet at the top, decrease the stitches together.

PROJECTS

SAMANTHA FRINGE TOP

SIZE

18–12 months, and 5–6

The specifications for the larger sizes are in parentheses. If there is only one specification, it applies to all sizes.

MATERIALS

Top shown worked in **Lana Grossa Soft Cotton**** (70% cotton, 30% acrylic, 153 yd / 1.8 oz) using the following colors and amounts:

02 Ecru: 1.8 oz
10 White: 1.8 oz
14 Cyclamen: 1.8 oz
27 Bright Orange: 1.8 oz
29 Turquoise: 1.8 oz
42 Curry: 1.8 oz
48 Opal Green: 1.8 oz

**If you have trouble finding this yarn, see the Conversion Chart on page 126 for substitutions.

Crochet hook G-6

GAUGE

1 square over 3 rounds = 2.8 in x 2.8 in, diagonal = 4 in x 4 in

1 square over 4 rounds = 3.5 in x 3.5 in, diagonal = 4.7 in x 4.7 in

PATTERN

Crochet square: Work 3 (4) rounds according to the crochet diagram. Work Round 1 around an adjustable foundation ring (= magic loop). For a neat transition crochet the slip stitch for closing the round in the new color.

Color sequence A: 1 round ecru, 1 round curry, 1 round cyclamen, 1 round turquoise

Color sequence B: 1 round white, 1 round bright orange, 1 round cyclamen, 1 round opal green

INSTRUCTIONS

Crochet 4 squares each over 3 (4) rounds in color sequences A and B.

Straps (2x): Crochet an 11.8-in-long chain of chain stitches in cyclamen.

ASSEMBLY

Sew the squares together from the right, using overcast stitches in turquoise around the back loops of the last round. Tie approximately 2.8-in-long fringes (= finished length) into the bottom edge of the top, using 4 threads of each color. Tie the straps to the top points of the back of the top. Thread each strap end through a top front point, and tie it to the other end.

TIP To avoid having to fasten off the tails, let them run along the back while crocheting, and crochet around them.

Diagram

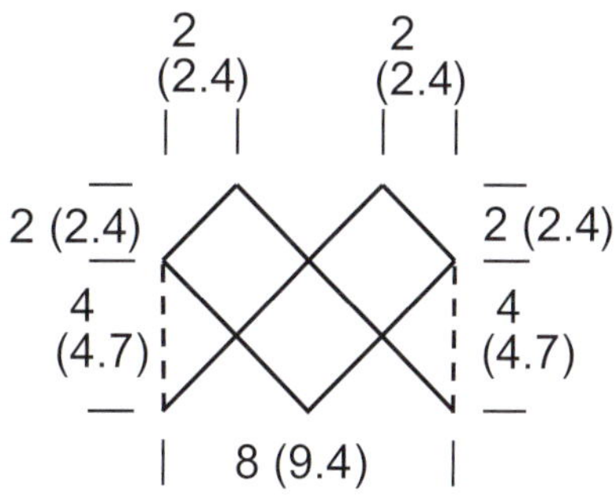

Crochet diagram

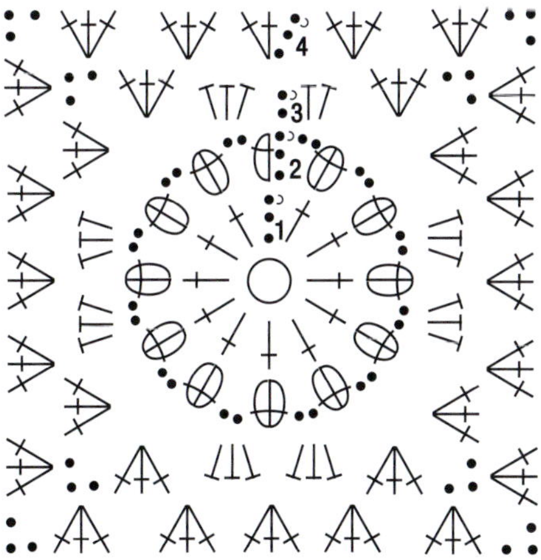

Key

• = 1 chain stitch

꜀ = 1 slip stitch

T = 1 half double crochet

† = 1 double crochet

(symbol) = 2 double crochets together

(symbol) = 3 double crochets together

If the symbols meet at the bottom, insert the hook into the same stitch. If the symbols meet at the top, decrease the stitches together.

JENNIFER TOP

SIZE

12–24 months, 3T–4T, and 5–6
The specifications for the larger sizes are in parentheses. If there is only one specification, it applies to all sizes.

MATERIALS

Top shown worked in **Junghans Wolle Recycle & PET**** (55% polyester, 45% cotton, 219 yd / 1.8 oz) using the following colors and amounts:
142-635 Fuchsia: 1.8 oz
142-636 Light Gray: 1.8 oz
142-637 Salmon: 3.5 oz (3.5 oz / 5 oz)
142-639 Wool White: 1.8 oz
**If you have trouble finding this yarn, see the Conversion Chart on page 126 for substitutions.

Crochet hook G-6

GAUGE

1 square over 4 rounds = 2.6 in x 2.6 in
1 square over 5 rounds = 2.9 in x 2.9 in
1 square over 6 rounds = 3.3 in x 3.3 in

PATTERNS

Crochet square: Work 4 (5 / 6) rounds according to the crochet diagram on p 21. Work Round 1 in wool white around an adjustable foundation ring (= magic loop). For a neat transition change the color before the decrease of the last half double crochet at the end of the round. Close the last round as shown for Round 5 in the diagram.

Single crochet: Begin each round with 1 turning chain, and close the round with 1 slip stitch in the 1st single crochet.

Color sequence: * 1 round wool white, 1 round light gray, 1 round fuchsia, repeat from *.

INSTRUCTIONS

Back and front: Crochet 8 squares each over 4 (5 / 6) rounds in the color sequence, working the last rounds each in salmon.

TIP To avoid having to fasten off the tails, let them run along the back while crocheting, and crochet around them.

ASSEMBLY

Crochet the squares together according to the diagram, using slip stitches in salmon from the right side and closing the side seams only over the bottom 4.7 in (5.3 in / 6 in). Work one round each of single crochet (number of stitches divisible by 6) and 1 round in salmon around the bottom of the top as follows: 1 chain stitch, * 1 single crochet, skip 2 stitches, (1 double crochet, 1 chain, 1 double crochet, 1 chain, 1 double crochet) in 1 stitch, skip 2 stitches, repeat from *, close the round with 1 slip stitch in the 1st single crochet. Crochet around the neckline and armholes in the same way, decreasing 2 single crochet together in each round in the corners at the neckline.

Diagram

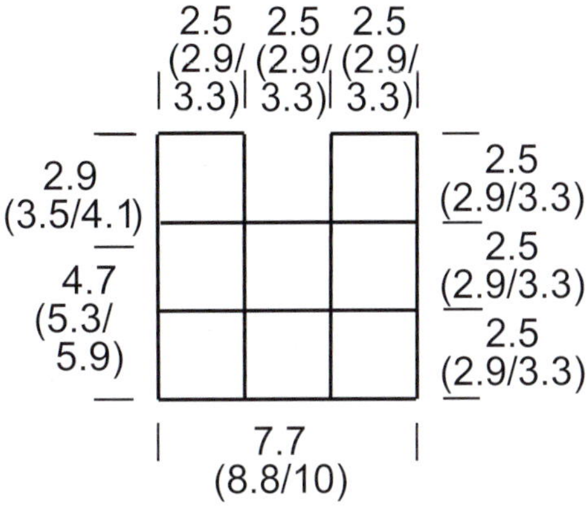
2.5 (2.9/ 3.3)
2.5 (2.9/ 3.3)
2.5 (2.9/ 3.3)
2.9 (3.5/4.1)
4.7 (5.3/ 5.9)
2.5 (2.9/3.3)
2.5 (2.9/3.3)
2.5 (2.9/3.3)
7.7 (8.8/10)

SAMMY PULLOVER

SIZE

12–24 months, and 3T–4T

The specifications for the larger sizes are in parentheses. If there is only one specification, it applies to all sizes.

MATERIALS

Pullover shown worked in **Schoeller + Stahl Limone**** (100% cotton, 137 yd / 1.8 oz) using the following colors and amounts:

06 Brilliant White: 5 oz

100 Yellow: 1.8 oz

108 Pink: 1.8 oz (3.5 oz)

197 Anemone: 1.8 oz

**If you have trouble finding this yarn, see the Conversion Chart on page 126 for substitutions.

Crochet hook D

GAUGE

1 square over 4 rounds = 2.8 in x 2.8 in

1 square over 5 rounds = 3.1 in x 3.1 in

PATTERN

Crochet square: Work 4 (5) rounds according to the crochet diagram on p 21. Crochet Round 1 in yellow around an adjustable foundation ring (= magic loop). For a neat transition change the color before the decrease of the last half double crochet at the end of the round. Close the last round as shown for Round 5 in the diagram.

Front and back double crochet: For front and back double crochet don't insert the hook into the stitch of the previous row or round, but guide it around the vertical loop of the lower stitch. Inserting the hook from front to back creates a front post double crochet; inserting the hook from back to front creates a back post double crochet.

Rib pattern in rounds (uneven number of stitches): Round 1: 1 chain stitch, work single crochet, close the round with 1 slip stitch in the 1st single crochet. Round 2: 3 turning chains (to replace the 1st double crochet), work double crochet, close the round with 1 slip stitch in the topmost turning chain. Round 3: 2 turning chains, * 1 front post double crochet, 1 back post double crochet, repeat from *, 1 front post double crochet, close the round with 1 slip stitch in the topmost turning chain. Work Rounds 1–3 1x, then keep repeating Round 3.

Color sequence: 1 round yellow, 1 round anemone, 1 round pink, 1 (2) round(s) brilliant white

INSTRUCTIONS

Front and back: Crochet 9 squares over 4 (5) rounds in the color sequence.

Shoulder yoke: Crochet 2 squares over 4 (5) rounds in the color sequence.

Side part (2x): Crochet 2 squares each over 4 (5) rounds in the color sequence.

Sleeves (2x): Crochet 6 squares each over 4 (5) rounds in the color sequence.

ASSEMBLY

Crochet the squares together according to the diagram, using slip stitches in brilliant white from the right side. Observe the fitting marks on the sleeve, and ensure that the 2 squares each of the shoulder yoke and the sides belong half to the front and half to the back. Crochet 4 rounds in brilliant white in rib pattern around the neckline. For the waistband crochet 6 rounds in brilliant white in rib pattern around the bottom edge of the sweater.

TIP To avoid having to fasten off the tails, let them run along the back while crocheting, and crochet around them.

Diagram

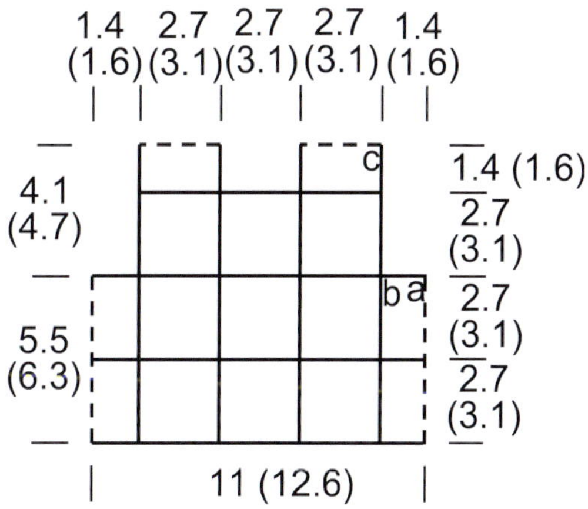

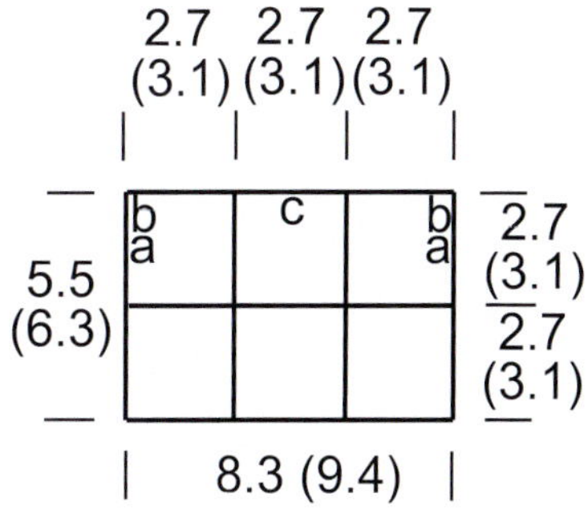

CAROLINE VEST

SIZE

3–9 months, 9–18 months, and 18–24 months
The specifications for the larger sizes are in parentheses. If there is only one specification, it applies to all sizes.

MATERIALS

Vest shown worked in **ONline Linie 107 Supersoft**** (60% cotton, 40% acrylic, 142 yd / 1.8 oz) using the following colors and amounts:
19 Natural: 1.8 oz (3.5 oz / 3.5 oz)
230 Coral: 1.8 oz
246 Vanilla: 1.8 oz
264 Apricot: 1.8 oz
**If you have trouble finding this yarn, see the Conversion Chart on page 126 for substitutions.

Crochet hook E-4

GAUGE

1 square over 4 rounds = 3.3 in x 3.3 in
1 square over 5 rounds = 4 in x 4 in
1 square over 6 rounds = 4.7 in x 4.7 in

PATTERN

Crochet square: Work 4 (5 / 6) according to the crochet diagram. Work Round 1 in coral around an adjustable foundation ring (= magic loop). For a neat transition crochet the slip stitch at the end of the round in the new color. Work Rounds 1–4 1x and the following rounds like Round 4, crocheting 1 double crochet cluster more per side.

Single crochet: Begin each round with 1 turning chain (it doesn't replace any stitch), and close the round with 1 slip stitch in the 1st single crochet.

Double crochet: Begin each round with 3 turning chains (to replace the 1st double crochet), and close the round with 1 slip stitch in the 3rd turning chain.

Color sequence: 1 round coral, 1 round apricot, 1 round vanilla, 1 (2 / 3) round(s) natural

INSTRUCTIONS

Back: Crochet 4 squares over 4 (5 / 6) rounds in the color sequence.

Left and right fronts: Crochet 2 squares each over 4 (5 / 6) rounds in the color sequence.

ASSEMBLY

Crochet the squares together according to the cut, using slip stitches in natural in the back loops only. Close the shoulder seams over 1.7 in (2 in / 2.4 in). Close the side seams over the bottom 3.3 in (4 in / 4.7 in). Crochet 1 round single crochets in natural around the outer edge of the vest, working 2 single crochets each in the corners. Crochet 1 round single crochets and 1 round double crochets each in natural around the armholes, working 3 double crochets each in 1 stitch in the 2nd round.

TIP To avoid having to fasten off the tails, let them run along the back while crocheting, and crochet around them.

Crochet diagram

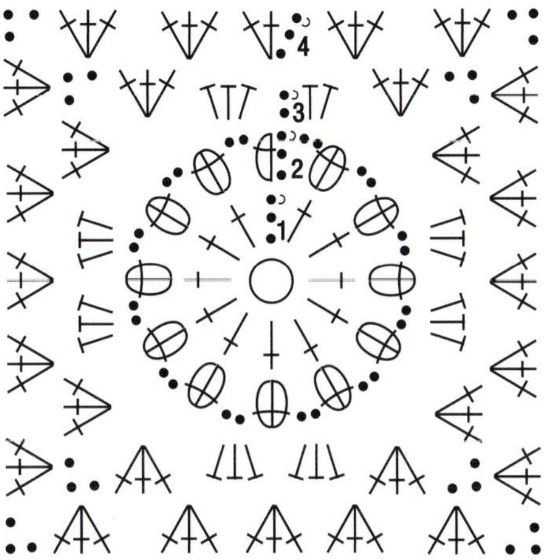

Diagram

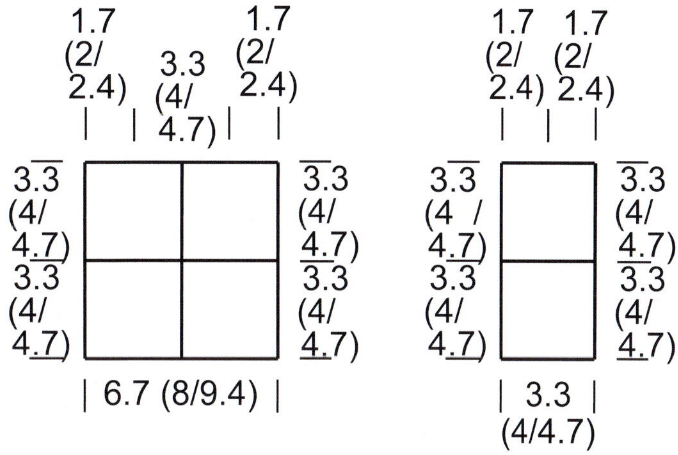

Key

- • = 1 chain stitch
- c = 1 slip stitch
- T = 1 half double crochet
- † = 1 double crochet
- = 2 double crochets together
- = 3 double crochets together

If the symbols meet at the bottom, insert the hook into the same stitch. If the symbols meet at the top, decrease the stitches together.

MADELYN TUNIC

SIZE

6–9 months, 24 months–3T, and 5–6
The specifications for the larger sizes are in parentheses. If there is only one specification, it applies to all sizes.

MATERIALS

Tunic shown worked in **Junghans Wolle Cotton Superfine II**** (100% cotton, 186 yd / 1.8 oz) using the following colors and amounts:
105-319 Ecru: 3.5 oz (5 oz / 5 oz)
109-641 Strawberry: 1.8 oz
139-597 Beige: 1.8 oz
139-599 Silver: 1.8 oz
139-490 Salmon: 1.8 oz
**If you have trouble finding this yarn, see the Conversion Chart on page 126 for substitutions.

Crochet hook E-4

GAUGE

1 square over 3 rounds = 2.4 in x 2.4 in
1 square over 4 rounds = 2.8 in x 2.8 in
1 square over 5 rounds = 3.3 in x 3.3 in
Double crochet pattern: 7 double crochet clusters and 13 rounds = 3.2 in x 4 in

PATTERN

Crochet square: Work 3 (4 / 5) rounds according to the crochet pattern on p 21. Crochet Round 1 around an adjustable foundation ring (= magic loop). For a neat transition change the color before decreasing the half double crochet at the end of the round. Close the last round as shown for Round 5 in the diagram.

Crochet triangle: Work 3 (4 / 5) rows according to the crochet diagram on p 23. Work Round 1 around an adjustable foundation ring (= magic loop).

Double crochet pattern in rounds: Round 1: 3 turning chains (to replace the 1st double crochet), 1 double crochet in the same stitch, * 3 double crochets between the 3 double crochets of the previous round, keep repeating from *, 1 double crochet in the same stitch as the 1st double crochet, close the round with 1 slip stitch in the topmost turning chain. Round 2: 3 turning chains (to replace the 1st double crochet), * 3 double crochets between the 3 double crochets of the previous round, keep repeating from *, close the round with 1 slip stitch in the topmost turning chain. Keep repeating Rounds 1 and 2.

INSTRUCTIONS

Back: Crochet 12 squares over 3 (4 / 5) rounds in the desired color sequence, working the last round each either in ecru, silver, or beige.

Right and left fronts: Crochet 5 squares each and 1 triangle each over 3 (4 / 5) rounds / rows in the desired color sequence, working the last round / row each either in ecru, silver, or beige.

TIP To avoid having to fasten off the tails, let them run along the back while crocheting, and crochet around them.

Assembling: Crochet the squares together in ecru from the right according to the diagram, using slip stitches. Leave 3.5 in (4.1 in / 4.9 in) open for the armholes.
Crochet 1 row single crochet in ecru each around the slit and the neckline and 1 row in ecru each as follows: over the bottom 2 squares each * 1 single crochet, skip 2 single crochet with 3 chain stitches, keep repeating from *, over the stitches of the neckline ** 1 single crochet, skip 2 stitches, 5 double crochets in 1 stitch, skip 2 stitches, keep repeating from **.
Crochet 1 round double crochets in ecru each around the armholes and 1 round in ecru each as follows: * 1 single crochet in 1 space, 5 double crochets in 1 space, keep repeating from *, close the round with 1 slip stitch in the 1st single crochet.

Skirt: Crochet double crochets in ecru around the bottom edge of the top, laying the slit edging on top of each other, and chaining in the 1st round at a side seam. To give it shape, increase 8 double crochet clusters evenly 1x in the 2nd round and 1x in the following 3rd round. Instead of 3 double crochets in a space, work 6 double crochets in a space. In the following round work 1 double crochet cluster in the center of each of these 6 double crochets. After 7.5 in (7.9 in / 8.1 in) = 25 (26 / 27) rounds work another 5 rounds in the desired color sequence from the beginning of the double crochet pattern. Finish the work.

ASSEMBLY

Chain an approximately 27.5 in (31 in / 35 in) long row of chain stitches in strawberry, and pull into the chain spaces of the slit.

Diagram

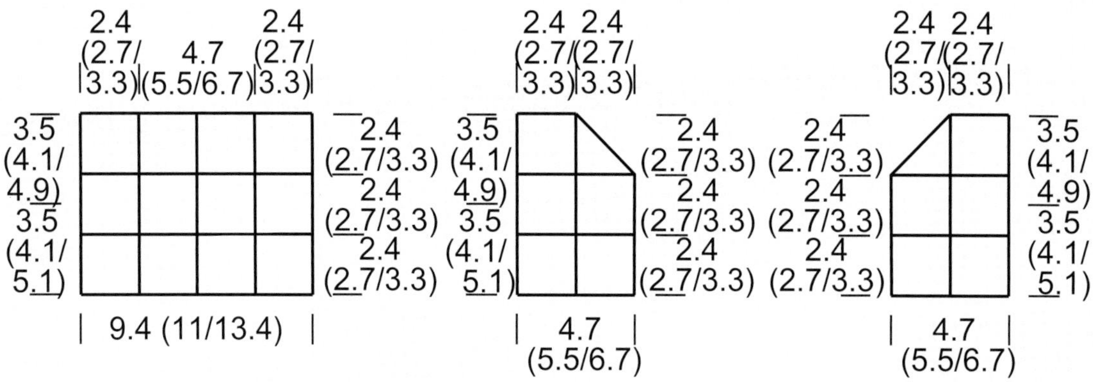

DECLAN SWEATER

SIZE

12–24 months, 24 months–3T, and 3T–5
The specifications for the larger sizes are in parentheses. If there is only one specification, it applies to all sizes.

MATERIALS

Sweater shown worked in **Austermann Baby Cotton**** (100% cotton, 197 yd / 1.8 oz) using the following colors and amounts:
02 Black: 1.8 oz
06 Taupe: 1.8 oz
07 Flecked Gray: 1.8 oz
10 Natural: 1.8 oz
22 Tangerine: 1.8 oz
23 Corn Yellow: 1.8 oz
25 Fjord: 5 oz (5 oz / 7 oz)
**If you have trouble finding this yarn, see the Conversion Chart on page 125 for substitutions.

Crochet hook D

GAUGE

1 square over 6 rounds = 3.5 in x 3.5 in
27 double crochets over 12 rows / rounds = 4 in x 4 in

PATTERN

Crochet square: Work 6 rounds according to the crochet pattern. Work Round 1 around an adjustable foundation ring (= magic loop). For a neat transition change the color before the slip stitch at the end of the round. If the symbols meet at the bottom, insert the hook into the same stitch.

Double crochet: Begin each row with 3 turning chains (to replace the 1st double crochet). Begin each round with 3 turning chains (to replace the 1st double crochet), and close the round with 1 slip stitch in the topmost turning chain.

Single crochet: Begin each row with 1 turning chain (it doesn't replace any stitch). Begin each round with 1 turning chain (it doesn't replace any stitch), and close the round with 1 slip stitch in the 1st single crochet.

Front and back post double crochet: For front and back post double crochet don't insert the hook into the stitch of the previous row or round, but guide it around the vertical loop of the lower stitch. Inserting the hook from front to back creates a front post double crochet; inserting the hook from back to front creates a back post double crochet.

Rib pattern in rows (uneven number of stitches): Row 1 = right side row: 1 turning chain (it doesn't replace any stitch), work single crochets. Row 2 = wrong side row: 3 turning chains (to replace the 1st double crochet), work double crochets. Row 3: 2 turning chains, * 1 front post double crochet, 1 back post double crochet, keep repeating from *, 1 front post double crochet. Row 4: 2 turning chains (to replace the 1st front post double crochet), * 1 back post double crochet, 1 front post double crochet, keep repeating from *, 1 back post double crochet. Work Rows 1–4 1x, then keep repeating Rows 3 and 4.

Rib pattern in rounds (uneven number of stitches): Round 1: 1 turning chain (it doesn't replace any stitch), work single crochets, close the round with 1 slip stitch in the 1st stitch. Round 2: 3 turning chains (to replace the 1st double crochet), work double crochets, close the round with 1 slip stitch in the topmost turning chain. Round 3: 2 turning chains (to replace the 1st double crochet), * 1 front post double crochet, 1 back post double crochet, keep repeating from *, close the round with 1 slip stitch in the topmost turning chain. Work Rounds 1–3 1x, then keep repeating Round 3.

INSTRUCTIONS

Elephant: Crochet 1 square over 6 rounds, working 4 rounds in flecked gray and 2 rounds in fjord.

Trunk: Work in flecked gray around an adjustable foundation ring. Round 1: 4 single crochets. Round 2: 2 single crochets in 1 stitch, 3 single crochets = 5 single crochets. Round 3: 2 single crochets, 2 single crochets in 1 stitch, 2 single crochets = 6 single crochets. Round 4: 2 single crochets in 1 stitch, 5 single crochets = 7 single crochets. Round 5: 7 single crochets. Round 6: 4 single crochets, 2 single crochets in 1 stitch, 2 single crochets = 8 single crochets. Rounds 7–12: 8 single crochets. Fold the work in half, and crochet the last round together with 4 single crochets. Finish the work.

Ear (2x): Work in taupe around an adjustable foundation ring. Round 1: 6 single crochets. Round 2: * 2 half double crochets in 1 stitch, 2x 2 single crochets each in 1 stitch, work 2x from *. Round 3, flecked gray: 6 single crochets, 6x double crochets each in 1 stitch, close the round with 1 slip stitch in the 1st single crochet. Finish the work.

Tusk (2x): Chain 5 chain stitches in natural, and crochet 1 row single crochets. Finish the work.

Eye (2x): Work in black around an adjustable foundation ring. Round 1: 4 single crochets. Finish the work.

Assemble the Elephant: Sew on the ears, trunk, eyes, and tusks (see photo). Stitch one point of light each in natural in the eyes.

Rhino: Crochet 1 square over 6 rounds, working 4 rounds in taupe and 2 rounds in fjord.

Snout: Work in taupe around an adjustable foundation ring. Round 1: 12 double crochets. Round 2: 2 single crochets each in 1 stitch = 24 single crochets. Finish the work.

Horn: Chain 5 chain stitches in natural. Round 1: 1 single crochet, 1 half double crochet, 1 double crochet, and 1 treble crochet. Finish the work.

Ear (2x): Work in taupe around an adjustable foundation ring. Round 1: 1 single crochet, 2 half double crochets, 2 double crochets, 1 treble crochet. Finish the work.

Eye (2x): Work in black around an adjustable foundation ring. Round 1: 4 single crochets. Finish the work.

Assemble the Rhino: Sew on the ears, horn, eyes, and snout (see photo). Stitch one point of light each in natural in the eyes and 2 nostrils in black on the snout (1 puff stitch each).

Giraffe: Crochet 1 square over 6 rounds, working 4 rounds in corn yellow and 2 rounds in fjord.

Snout: Work around an adjustable foundation ring. Round 1: 12 double crochets. Round 2: 2 single crochets each in 1 stitch = 24 single crochets. Finish the work.

Horn (2x): Chain 6 chain stitches in corn yellow. Round 1: 5 single crochets. Round 2: 5 slip stitches. Round 3, taupe: (1 chain stitch, 1 single crochet, 1 half double crochet, 1 double crochet, 1 half double crochet, 1 single crochet, 1 slip stitch) around the tip of the 1st round.

Ear (2x): Work in corn yellow around an adjustable foundation ring. Round 1: 1 single crochet, 2 half double crochets, 2 double crochets, 1 treble crochet. Finish the work.

Eye (2x): Work in black around an adjustable foundation ring. Round 1: 4 single crochets. Finish the work.

Spots (4x): Work in taupe around an adjustable foundation ring. Round 1: 6 single crochets. Round 2: 3x 2 single crochets each in 1 stitch, leave the remaining stitches unworked. Finish the work.
Assemble the Giraffe: Sew on the ears, snout, eyes, horns, and spots (see photo). Stitch one point of light each in natural in the eyes and 2 nostrils in black on the snout (1 moss stitch each).

Tiger: Crochet 1 square over 6 rounds, working 4 rounds in tangerine and 2 rounds in fjord.
Cheek (2x): Work in natural around an adjustable foundation. Round 1: 6 single crochets. Round 2: Keep alternating between 1 slip stitch and 1 chain stitch. Finish the work.
Snout: Chain 5 chain stitches in taupe. Round 1: 2 double crochets together. Finish the work.
Ear (2x): Chain 6 chain stitches in tangerine. Round 1: 5 slip stitches. Round 2: 4 chains, 4 treble crochets together. Finish the work.
Eye (2x): Work in black around an adjustable foundation ring. Round 1: 4 single crochets. Finish the work.
Assemble the Tiger: Sew on the ears, snout, eyes and cheeks (see photo). Stitch one point of light each in natural in the eyes and lines in black on the head (see photo).

TIP To avoid having to fasten off the tails, let them run along the back while crocheting, and crochet around them.

Assembly: Sew the squares together from the right side according to the diagram, using overcast stitches in fjord around the back loops of the last round.

Front: Crochet another 1 in (1.2 in / 1.4 in) = 2 (3 / 4) rounds double crochets in fjord around the squares, working the corners as in the last round of the crochet diagram. Crochet a further 1 in (1.2 in / 1.4 in) = 3 (3 / 3) rows double crochets in fjord on both sides.
Continue working rows of double crochets in fjord over the top edge, skipping the middle 27 (31 / 35) stitches in the 1st round for the neckline and finishing both sides separately. For the neckline slant work 2 double crochets each together 3x on the inner edge in each row. Finish the work after another 1.6 in = 5 rows from the beginning of the neckline.

Back: Chain 73 (79 / 85) chain stitches in fjord, and work double crochets. For the neckline skip the middle 33 (37 / 41) double crochets after 10 in (11 in / 11.6 in) = 31 (34 / 35) rows from the waistband, and finish both sides separately. Finish the work after 11.4 in (12 in / 12.6 in) = 35 (37 / 38) rounds from the waistband.

Sleeves (2x): Chain 45 (49 / 53) chain stitches in fjord, and work 1.2 in = 7 rows in rib pattern for the wristband. Continue working double crochets. For the sleeve caps increase 1 double crochet each 7x (8x / 9x) = 59 (65 / 71) double crochets in every 3rd row on both sides. Finish the work after 8 in (8.9 in / 9.6 in) = 24 (27 / 29) rows from the beginning of the wristband.

ASSEMBLY

Close the shoulder seams. Crochet 0.8 in = 5 rounds in rib pattern in fjord around the neckline. Insert the sleeves, and close the sleeve and side seams.

Crochet diagram

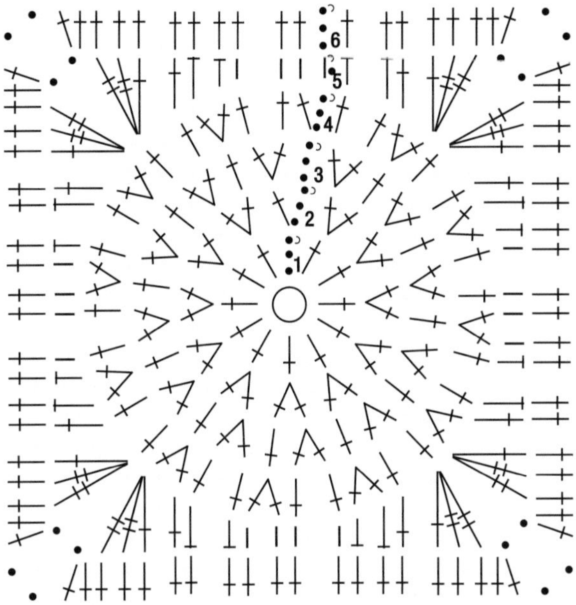

Key

- • = 1 chain stitch
- ◦ = 1 slip stitch
- | = 1 single crochet
- T = 1 half double crochet
- † = 1 double crochet
- ǂ = 1 treble crochet

If the symbols meet at the bottom, insert the hook into the same stitch. If the symbols meet at the top, decrease the stitches together.

Diagram

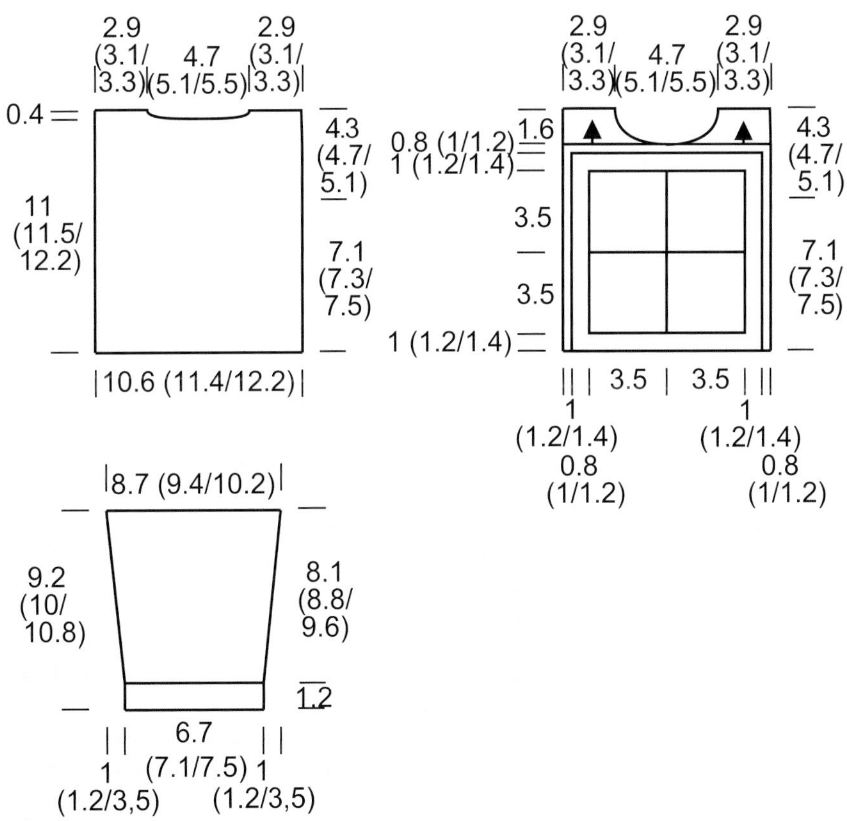

DELILAH DRESS AND HAIRBAND

SIZE

18–24 months, 3T–4T, and 5–6
The specifications for the larger sizes are in parentheses. If there is only one specification, it applies to all sizes.

MATERIALS

Dress and Hairband shown worked in **Lang Yarns Baby Cotton**** (100% cotton, 197 yd / 1.8 oz) using the following amounts and colors:
0007 Lilac: 1.8 oz
0028 Apricot: 1.8 oz
0033 Blue: 1.8 oz
0044 Lime: 1.8 oz
0048 Pale Red: 1.8 oz
0091 Pale Green: 1.8 oz
0096 Beige: 5 oz (7 oz / 7 oz)
0178 Indigo: 1.8 oz
0246 Violet: 1.8 oz
**If you have trouble finding this yarn, see the Conversion Chart on page 126 for substitutions.

Crochet hook D

GAUGE

1 square over 7 rounds = 4.1 in x 4.1 in
Double crochet pattern: 10 double crochet clusters and 20 rows / rounds = 4.7 in x 5.1 in

PATTERN

Crochet square: Work according to the crochet diagram on p 21. Work Round 1 around an adjustable foundation ring (= magic loop). For a neat transition change the color before decreasing the half double crochet at the end of the round. Close the last round as shown for Round 5 in the diagram.

Double crochet pattern in rows: Row 1: 3 turning chains (to replace the 1st double crochet), 1 double crochet in the same stitch, * 3 double crochets between the 3 double crochets of the previous row, keep repeating from *, 2 double crochets around the corner chain stitches or the topmost turning chain. Row 2: 3 turning chains (to replace the 1st double crochet), * 3 double crochets between the 3 crochets of the previous row, keep repeating from *, 1 double crochet. Keep repeating Rows 1 and 2.

Double crochet pattern in rounds: Round 1: 3 turning chains (to replace the 1st double crochet), 1 double crochet in the same stitch, * 3 double crochets between the 3 double crochets of the previous round, keep repeating from *, 1 double crochet in the same stitch as the 1st double crochet, close the round with 1 slip stitch in the topmost turning chain. Round 2: 3 turning chains (to replace the 1st double crochet), * 3 double crochets between the 3 double crochets of the previous round, keep repeating from *, close the round with 1 slip stitch in the topmost turning chain. Keep repeating Rounds 1 and 2.

Single crochet: Begin each round with 1 turning chain (it doesn't replace any stitch).

Color sequence A: 1 round beige, 1 round apricot, 1 round blue, 1 round pale green, 1 round beige, 1 round lilac, 1 round pale red, 1 round indigo, 1 round beige, 1 round lime, 1 round violet, 1 round apricot, 1 (2 / 3) round(s) beige

Color sequence B: 16 (19 / 22) rounds beige, 1 round apricot, 1 round blue, 1 round pale green, 1 round beige, 1 round lilac, 1 round pale red, 1 round indigo, 1 round beige, 1 round lime, 1 round violet, 1 round apricot, 1 round beige, 1 round blue, 1 round pale green, 1 round lilac, 1 round beige, 1 round pale red, 1 round indigo, 1 round lime, 3 rounds beige

DRESS

INSTRUCTIONS

Top (2x): Crochet 1 square over 13 (14 / 15) rounds in color sequence A; don't cut the yarn after the last round. Crochet 2 rows in double crochet pattern in beige over one side of the square. Also crochet 2 rows in double crochet pattern in beige over the opposite side of the square.

Assembly: Close the side seams, crocheting them together with slip stitches in beige from the right side.

Skirt: Crochet around the bottom edge of the top in double crochet pattern in color sequence B, chaining in Round 1 at a side seam and working 1 double crochet cluster each in every 2nd row of the side double crochet pattern. To give it shape, work 1 double crochet cluster each 5x evenly distributed in every 2nd round and in the center of these 6 double crochets in the following round. Then crochet 1 more round in shell pattern: 1 single crochet, * 5 double crochets in the following gap, 1 single crochet in the following gap, keep repeating from *, close the round with 1 single crochet in the 1st single crochet. If necessary, crochet 3 double crochets in the last free gap at the end of the round. Finish the work.

Strap (4x): Chain 53 chain stitches in beige. Round 1: 1 single crochet in the 2nd chain from the hook, * skip 2 chains, 5 double crochets in 1 chain, skip 2 chains, 1 single crochet in 1 chain, work 8x from *, skip 2 chains, 10 double crochets in 1 chain, now carry on working on the other side of the chain stitch chain, ** skip 2 chains, 1 single crochet in 1 chain, skip 2 chains, 5 double crochets in 1 chain, work 8x from **, skip 2 chains, 1 single crochet in 1 chain. Finish the work.

TIP To avoid having to fasten off the tails, let them run along the back while crocheting, and crochet around them.

ASSEMBLY

Sew the straps onto the top edge of the top, and knot together on the shoulders.

Diagram

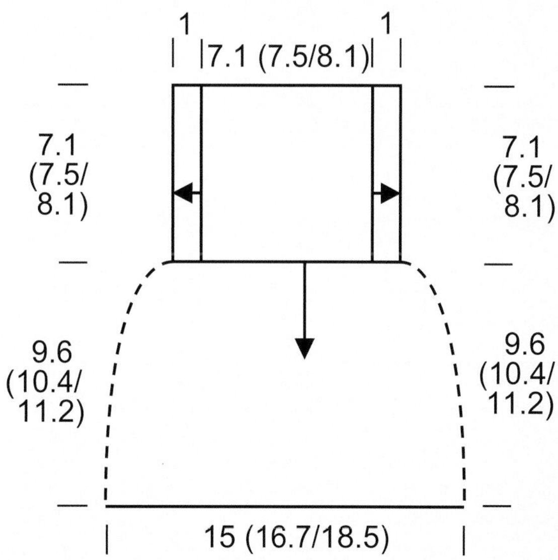

HAIRBAND

INSTRUCTIONS

Crochet 3 (3 / 5) squares over 4 rounds in the desired color sequence, working the last round in beige.

ASSEMBLY

Crochet the squares together in a row with slip stitches in beige from the right. Work 1 row single crochets each in beige around the long sides. Crochet 5 rows each in double crochet pattern around the short sides, working 1 half double crochet cluster less from Row 2 and then in every following row on both sides—meaning, work slip stitches at the beginning of the row until the first gap, and leave the remaining stitches at the end of the row and after the last gap as they are. For tying the hairband, chain 45 chain stitches. Finish the work.

BENJAMIN JACKET

SIZE

12–24 months and 1½–3T

The specifications for the larger sizes are in parentheses. If there is only one specification, it applies to all sizes.

MATERIALS

Jacket shown worked in **Austermann Merino 120**** (100% pure wool, 131 yd / 1.8 oz) using the following colors and amounts:

104 Navy: 3.5 oz
110 Natural: 1.8 oz
123 Jeans Blue: 1.8 oz
132 Royal Blue: 3.5oz
133 Petrol Blue: 1.8 oz
140 Absinthe: 1.8 oz
162 Blue Curaçao: 1.8 oz
170 Olive: 1.8 oz
173 Grass Green: 1.8 oz
175 Lemon: 1.8 oz

**If you have trouble finding this yarn, see the Conversion Chart on page 125 for substitutions.

Crochet hook G-6
5 buttons

GAUGE

1 square over 3 rounds = 2.6 in x 2.6 in
1 square over 4 rounds = 3.2 in x 3.2 in

PATTERN

Crochet square: Work 3 (4) rounds according to the crochet diagram on p 21. Work Round 1 around an adjustable foundation ring (= magic loop). For a neat transition change the color before decreasing the half double crochet at the end of the round. Close the last round as shown for Round 5 in the diagram.

Crochet triangle: Work 3 (4) rows according to the crochet diagram on p 23. Work Row 1 around an adjustable foundation ring (= magic loop).

Front and back post double crochet: For front and back post double crochets, don't insert the hook into the stitch of the previous row or round, but guide it around the vertical loop of the lower stitch. Inserting the hook from front to back creates a front post double crochet; inserting the hook from back to front creates a back post double crochet.

Rib pattern in rows (uneven number of stitches): Row 1 = right side row: 1 chain stitch, work single crochets. Row 2 = wrong side row: 2 turning chains (to replace the 1st front post double crochet), * 1 front post double crochet, 1 back post double crochet, keep repeating from *, 1 front post double crochet. Row 3: 2 turning chains (to replace the 1st front post double crochet), * 1 back post double crochet, 1 front post double crochet, keep repeating from *, 1 back post double crochet. Work Rows 1–3 1x, then keep repeating Rows 3 and 4.

INSTRUCTIONS

Back: Crochet 16 squares over 3 (4) rounds in the desired color sequence, working the last rounds of 8 squares each in navy and royal blue.

Diagram

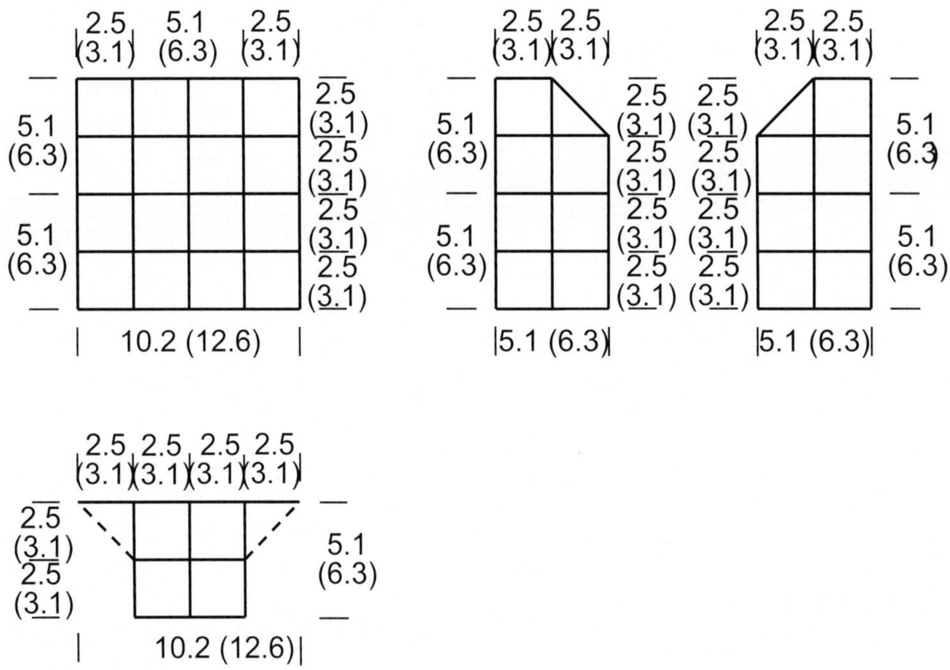

Left front: Crochet 7 squares and 1 triangle each over 3 (4) rows / rounds in the desired color sequence, working the last rounds of 3 squares and 1 triangle in navy and the last rounds of 4 squares in royal blue.

Right front: Crochet 7 squares and 1 triangle each over 3 (4) rows / rounds in the desired color sequence, working the last rounds of 3 squares and 1 triangle in royal blue and the last rounds of 4 squares in navy.

Left sleeve (2x): Crochet 5 squares each over 3 (4) rounds in the desired color sequence, working the last rounds of 2 squares each in navy and the last round of the triangle in royal blue.

Right sleeve (2x): Crochet 5 squares each over 3 (4) rounds in the desired color sequence, working the last rounds of 2 squares each in navy and royal blue and the last round of the triangle in navy.

ASSEMBLY

Crochet the squares together with slip stitches in royal blue from the right side according to the diagram. Close the shoulder seams. Crochet 4 rows slip stitches in rib pattern in navy and 1 row slip stitches in royal blue around the finished edges of the fronts and the back neckline, working 5 buttonholes (= skip 1 double crochet with 1 chain stitch; in the following row, work 1 double crochet around the chain) evenly in the 3rd row of the facing of the left top to the beginning of the slanted neckline. Insert the sleeves, folding one square diagonally in half. Close the arm and side seams by crocheting them together with slip stitches in royal blue from the right side.

NOTE: To lengthen the sleeves or the jacket, you can crochet a facing around the bottom edges.

TIP To avoid having to fasten off the tails, let them run along the back while crocheting, and crochet around them.

ROO PANTS

SIZE

3–9 months, 9–18 months, and 18–24 months
The specifications for the larger sizes are in parentheses. If there is only one specification, it applies to all sizes.

MATERIALS

Pants shown worked in **Buttinette Woll Butt Primo Madeleine**** (100% pure wool, 164 yd / 1.8 oz) using the following colors and amounts:
99.103.822 Heather: 1.8 oz
99.142.42 Multicolored: 1.8 oz
99.229.93 Taupe: 3.5 oz (3.5 oz / 5 oz)
99.240.89 Camel: 1.8 oz
99.378.32 Dark Red: 1.8 oz
99.381.37 Bordeaux: 1.8 oz
99.381.46: Terracotta
**If you have trouble finding this yarn, see the Conversion Chart on page 125 for substitutions.

Crochet hook E-4

GAUGE

1 square over 6 rounds = 4 in x 4 in

PATTERN

Crochet square: Work 14 (16 / 18) rounds according to the crochet diagram on p 21. Work Round 1 around an adjustable foundation ring (= magic loop). For a neat transition change the color before decreasing the half double crochet at the end of the round. Close the last round as shown for Round 5 in the diagram.

Double crochet pattern: Row 1: 3 turning chains (to replace the 1st double crochet), 1 double crochet in the same stitch, * 3 double crochets between the 3 double crochets of the previous row, keep repeating from *, 2 double crochets around the corner chain stitches or the topmost turning chain. Row 2: 3 turning chains (to replace the 1st double crochet), * 3 double crochets between the 3 double crochets of the previous row, keep repeating from *, 1 double crochet. Keep repeating Rows 1 and 2.

Front and back post double crochet: For front and back post double crochet, don't insert the hook into the stitch of the previous row or round, but guide it around the vertical loop of the lower stitch. Inserting the hook from front to back creates a front post double crochet; inserting the hook from back to front creates a back post double crochet.

Rib pattern in rounds (uneven number of stitches): Round 1: 1 turning chain (it doesn't replace any stitch), work single crochets, close the round with 1 slip stitch in the 1st single crochet. Round 2: 3 turning chains (to replace the 1st double crochet), work double crochets, close the round with 1 slip stitch in the 1st topmost turning chain. Round 3: 2 turning chains (to replace the 1st front post double crochet), * 1 front post double crochet, 1 back post double crochet, keep repeating from *, close the round with 1 slip stitch in the 1st topmost turning chain. Work Rounds 1–3 1x, then keep repeating Round 3.

Color sequence: * 1 round camel, 1 round bordeaux, 1 round terracotta, 1 round multicolored, 1 round dark red, 1 round taupe, 1 round heather, repeat from *.

INSTRUCTIONS

Trouser legs (2x): Crochet 1 square over 14 (16 / 18) rounds in the color sequence. For the crotch work 1 round double crochets in taupe to the middle of the following side. Finish the work. Work the opposite crotch in the opposite direction.

ASSEMBLY

Close the crotch seam by crocheting together slip stitches in taupe from the right side. Close the pants leg seams with overcast stitches in the respective color in the back loops of the last round. Crochet 2.8 in = 13 rounds in rib pattern around the upper edge of the pants.
Chain 26 in (28 in / 30 in) of chain stitches in dark red, and pull into the middle of the waistband.

TIP To avoid having to fasten off the tails, let them run along the back while crocheting, and crochet around them.

Diagram

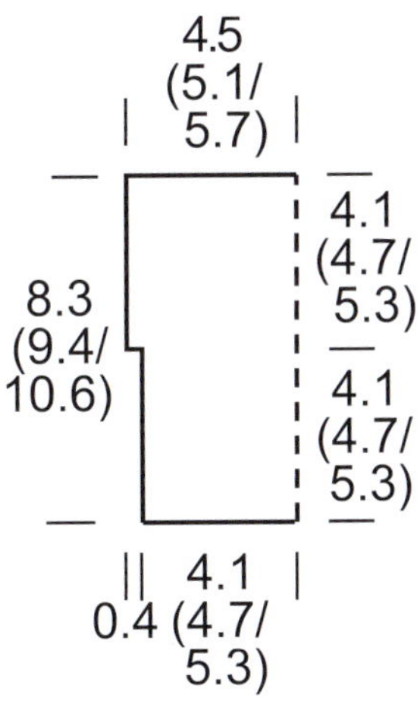

BABY JESS OVERALLS

SIZE

3-9 months, 9–18 months, and 18–24 months
The specifications for the larger sizes are in parentheses. If there is only one specification, it applies to all sizes.

MATERIALS

Overalls shown worked in **Buttinette Woll Butt Camilla**** (100% cotton, 137 yd / 1.8 oz) using the following colors and amounts:
103.768 Navy: 1.8 oz
103.769 Natural: 1.8 oz
240.39 Aqua: 1.8 oz
354.34: Turquoise: 1.8 oz
354.38 Pale Green: 1.8 oz each
354.41 Gray: 3.5 oz
354.44 Royal Blue: 1.8 oz
**If you have trouble finding this yarn, see the Conversion Chart on page 125 for substitutions.

Crochet hook D
2 Buttons, 0.6 in

GAUGE

1 square over 3 rounds = 2 in x 2 in
1 square over 4 rounds = 2.6 in x 2.6 in
1 square over 5 rounds = 3.2 in x 3.2 in
1 square over 7 rounds = 4.1 in x 4.1 in

PATTERN

Crochet square: Work rounds according to the crochet diagram on p 21. Work Round 1 around an adjustable foundation ring (= magic loop). For a neat transition change the color before decreasing the half double crochet at the end of the round. Close the last round as shown for Round 5 in the diagram.

Double crochet: Begin each row with 3 turning chains (to replace the 1st double crochet). Begin each round with 3 turning chains (to replace the 1st double crochet), and close the round with 1 slip stitch in the topmost turning chain.

INSTRUCTIONS

Trouser leg (2x): Crochet 12 squares each over 3 (4 / 5) rounds in the desired color sequence, working the last rounds each in gray.

Bib: Crochet 1 square over 8 (9 / 10) rounds in the desired color sequence, working the last round in gray.

Strap (2x): Chain 83 chain stitches in gray, and crochet 2 rows double crochets. Crochet a further 5 chains at the narrow edge, and close these with 1 slip stitch at the chain at the beginning to create a buttonhole loop.

ASSEMBLY

Crochet the squares of the pants legs together according to the diagram, working slip stitches in gray from the right side. Close the crotch seam with slip stitches in gray from the right side. Crochet 1 round double crochets in gray around the top edge of the pants. Crochet the bib from the right in the center to the top edge of the front pants, working slip stitches in gray. Sew the buttons onto the top corners of the bib.

Sew the straps onto the top back edge, cross once, and fasten to the bib with the buttons. Make a 30 in (33 in / 37 in) long cord from a total of 4 yarns in royal blue, and pull into the double crochet round at the top edge of the legs.

TIP To avoid having to fasten off the tails, let them run along the back while crocheting, and crochet around them.

Diagram

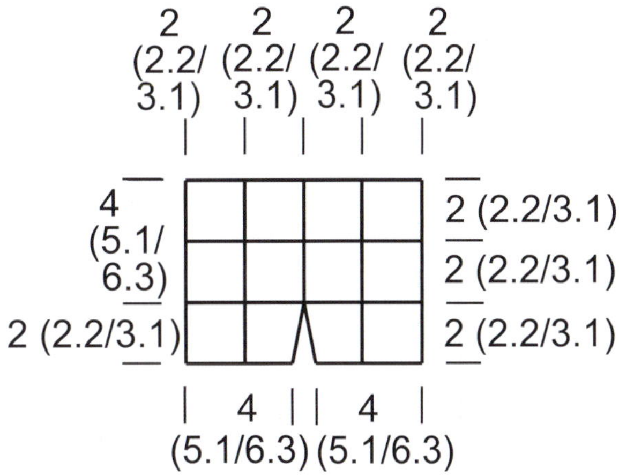

KATIE DRESS AND HAT

SIZE

3–9 months, 9–18 months, and 18–24 months
The specifications for the larger sizes are in parentheses. If there is only one specification, it applies to all sizes.

MATERIALS

Dress and Hat shown worked in **ONline Linie 23 Club**** (50% cotton, 50% viscose, 148 yd / 1.8 oz) using the following colors and amounts:
12 Yellow: 1.8 oz
16 Rose: 3.5 oz (5 oz / 5 oz)
21 Coral: 1.8 oz
28 Salmon: 1.8 oz
30 Raspberry: 1.8 oz
34 Vanilla: 1.8 oz
**If you have trouble finding this yarn, see the Conversion Chart on page 126 for substitutions.

Crochet hook E-4

GAUGE

1 square over 4 rounds = 3.2 in x 3.2 in
1 square over 5 rounds = 3.7 in x 3.7 in
1 square over 6 rounds = 4.3 in x 4.3 in
Double crochet pattern: 7 double crochet clusters and 13.5 rows / rounds = 4 in x 4 in

PATTERN

Crochet square: Work 4 (5 / 6) rounds according to the crochet diagram on p 27. Work Round 1 around an adjustable foundation ring (= magic loop). For a neat transition change the color before the slip stitch at the end of the round. Work Rounds 1–4 1x, then crochet the following rounds like Round 4, working 1 double crochet cluster more each per side.

Double crochet pattern in rounds: Round 1: 3 turning chains (to replace the 1st double crochet), 1 double crochet in the same stitch, * 3 double crochets between the 3 double crochets of the previous round, keep repeating from *, 1 double crochet in the same stitch as the 1st double crochet, close the round with 1 slip stitch in the topmost turning chain. Round 2: 3 turning chains (to replace the 1st double crochet), * 3 double crochets between the 3 double crochets of the previous round, keep repeating from *, close the round with 1 slip stitch in the topmost turning chain. Keep repeating Rounds 1 and 2.

Single crochet: Begin each round with 1 turning chain (it doesn't replace any stitch), and close the round with 1 slip stitch in the 1st single crochet.

Color sequence A (dress top): 1 round yellow, 1 round coral, 1 round vanilla, 1 (2 / 3) round(s) rose

Color sequence B (skirt): 4 (5 / 7) rounds rose, 4 (5 / 7) rounds salmon, 4 (5 / 7) rounds coral, 4 (5 / 7) rounds yellow, 1 round raspberry, 1 round pink, 1 round salmon, 1 round yellow, 1 round rose

Color sequence C (hat): 1 round yellow, 1 round coral, 1 round vanilla, 1 (2) round(s) rose

Color sequence D (brim): 4 rounds pink, 2 rounds raspberry, 1 round vanilla, 1 round rose

DRESS

INSTRUCTIONS

Top: Crochet 4 squares over 4 (5 / 6) rounds in color sequence A.

TIP To avoid having to fasten off the tails, let them run along the back while crocheting, and crochet around them.

Assembling: Crochet the squares together according to the diagram, using slip stitches in rose from the right side.

Skirt: Crochet around the bottom edge of the top in double crochet pattern in color sequence B. To give it shape, increase 4 double crochet clusters 3x (3x / 4x) in every 2nd round evenly distributed, working 6 double crochets each in a gap (instead of 3 double crochets each in a gap). In the following round, work 1 double crochet cluster each in the center of these 6 double crochets. Finish the work.

ASSEMBLE THE DRESS

Crochet 1 round reverse single crochets (= single crochets from left to right) in rose around the top edge of the dress.

Strap (4x): Work 3x per strap as follows (choose the colors you like): chain 60 (70 / 80) chain stitches after the reverse single crochet round at the top. Finish the work. Tie the ends of the chains together. Braid the 3 chains together, and knot the end.

Diagram

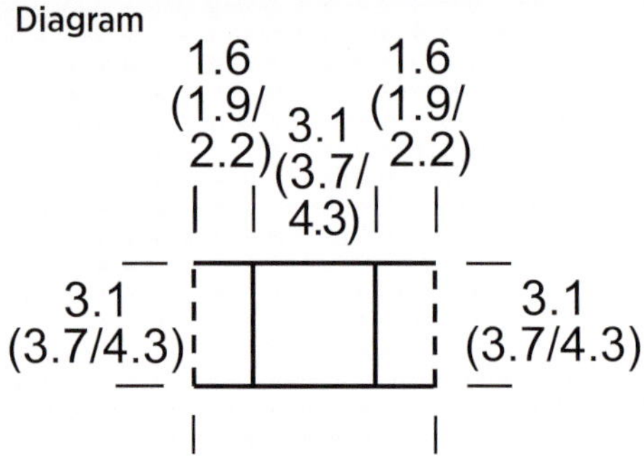

HAT

INSTRUCTIONS

Top: Crochet 5 squares over 4 (5) rounds in color sequence C.

ASSEMBLE THE HAT

Crochet 4 squares together to a ring, working slip stitches in rose from the right side. Crochet all sides of the 5th square in rose, working slip stitches from the right side in the center of a long crochet edge of the ring.

Brim: To ensure a stiff brim, keep working with two yarns, using an E-4 crochet hook. Work 5 rounds single crochets, 2 rounds half double crochets, and 1 round reverse single crochets in color sequence D. To shape the brim, increase 8 evenly spaced single crochets 2x in each round and increase 10 evenly spaced stitches 4x in each round.

REBECCA SKIRT

SIZE

4–5 years and 6–7 years

The specifications for the larger sizes are in parentheses. If there is only one specification, it applies to all sizes.

MATERIALS

Skirt shown worked in **Junghans Wolle Cotone-Emozione**** (50% cotton, 50% acrylic, 115 yd / 1.8 oz) using the following colors and amounts:

134-202 Heather: 1.8 oz
134-204 Lime: 1.8 oz
134-208 Orange: 1.8 oz
134-209 Red: 1.8 oz
137-182 White: 3.5 oz (5 oz)
137-183 Rose: 1.8 oz
139-486 Pink: 1.8 oz
142-667 Salmon: 1.8 oz
142-668 Grass Green: 1.8 oz

**If you have trouble finding this yarn, see the Conversion Chart on page 126 for substitutions.

Crochet hook G-6

GAUGE

1 square over 3 rounds = 2.4 in x 2.4 in
1 square over 4 rounds = 3 in x 3 in

PATTERN

Crochet square: Work 3 (4) rounds according to the crochet diagram on p 21. Work Round 1 around an adjustable foundation ring (= magic loop). For a neat transition change the color before decreasing the half double crochet at the end of the round. Close the last round as shown for Round 5 in the diagram.

Double crochet: Begin each round with 3 turning chains (to replace the 1st double crochet), and close the round with 1 slip stitch in the topmost turning chain.

Color sequence A (small squares over 3 rounds):
A1: 1 round heather, 1 round white, 1 round salmon
A2: 1 round rose, 1 round orange, 1 round grass-green
A3: 1 round salmon, 1 round red, 1 round lime
A4: 1 round lime, 1 round heather, 1 round white
A5: 1 round grass-green, 1 round pink, 1 round orange

Color sequence B (medium squares over 4 rounds):
B1: 1 round heather, 2 rounds white, 1 round salmon
B2: 1 round rose, 2 rounds orange, 1 round grass-green
B3: 1 round salmon 2 rounds red, 1 round lime
B4: 1 round lime, 2 rounds heather, 1 round white
B5: 1 round grass-green, 2 rounds pink, 1 round orange

INSTRUCTIONS

Crochet 8 (10) small squares over 3 rounds, with 2x each in the color sequences A1, A2, A3, and A4 (A1, A2, A3, A4, and A5). Then crochet 8 (10) medium-size squares each over 4 rounds, with 2x each in the color sequences B1, B2, B3, and B4 (B1, B2, B3, B4, and B5).

ASSEMBLY

Crochet together squares A1–4 (A1–5) and B1–4 (B1–5) in white from the right side to form 2 rings according to the diagram, paying attention to the order of the squares in the diagram (front and back are equal). Close the side seams.
For the waistband, crochet 3 rounds double crochets around the top edge of the ring made from the squares of color sequence A, crocheting 1 round each in white, orange, and white, and working 10 double crochets in each square in the 1st round.
Crochet 1 round each in white, red and orange (white, red, orange, lime, and pink) around the bottom edge of the ring made from the squares of color sequence A, working 12 double crochets in each square in the 1st round. To give it shape, increase 1 double crochet in each square (= 2 double crochets in 1 stitch) in Rounds 3 and 4 (2x in each 2nd round).
Next, crochet 1 round double crochets in white around the top edge of the ring made from the squares of color sequence B, working 14 double crochets in each square. Join this round with the last round of the top ring, working slip stitches in white from the right side.
Crochet 3 (5) rounds double crochets around the bottom edge of the ring made from the squares of color sequence B: 1 round each in white, grass-green, and white (white, grass-green, pink, salmon, and white), working 14 double crochets in each square in the 1st round. To give it shape, increase 1 double crochet in each square in Rounds 3 and 4 (2x in each 2nd round).
Finally, crochet 1 round reverse single crochets (= single crochets from left to right) in white.
Chain 180 (200) chain stitches in white, and pull into the 2nd round of the waistband. Tie a knot in each end.

TIP To avoid having to fasten off the tails, let them run along the back while crocheting, and crochet around them.

Note: You can lengthen the skirt by crocheting more double crochet rounds between the rings. You can also make a larger-size skirt by working more squares per ring.

Diagram

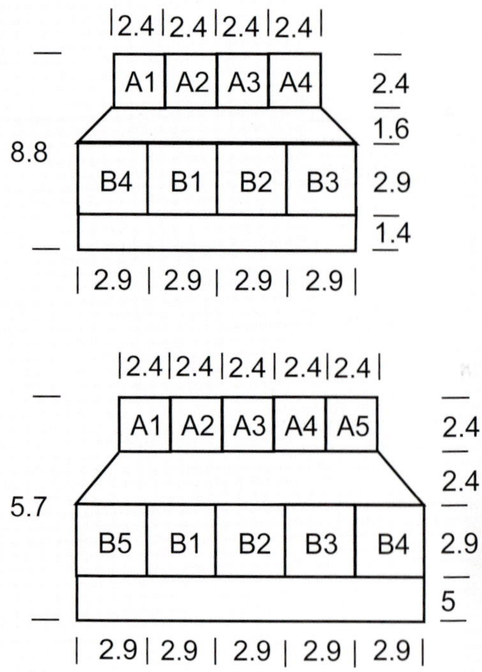

AMELIA PONCHO

SIZE

1½–3 T

MATERIALS

Poncho shown worked in **Lang Yarns Merino 120**** (100% pure wool, 131 yd / 1.8 oz) using the following colors and amounts:

0001 Natural: 1.8 oz	0226 Beige: 5 oz
0004 Black: 1.8 oz	0233 Blue: 1.8 oz
0091 Linden Green: 1.8 oz	0287 Dusty Pink: 1.8 oz
0098 Petrol Green: 1.8 oz	0297 Green: 1.8 oz
0098 Fir Green: 1.8 oz	0398 Moss: 1.8 oz
0129 Raspberry: 1.8 oz	0428 Apricot: 1.8 oz
0134 Pale Blue: 1.8 oz	0480 Bordeaux: 1.8 oz
0149 Yellow: 1.8 oz	0515 Terracotta: 1.8 oz
0174 Mint: 1.8 oz	0562 Red: 1.8 oz
0219 Pink: 1.8 oz	0566 Cyclamen: 1.8 oz

**If you have trouble finding this yarn, see the Conversion Chart on page 126 for substitutions.

Crochet hook G-6

GAUGE

1 square over 5 rounds = 3.3 in x 3.3 in, diagonal 4.7 in

PATTERN

Crochet square: Work 5 rounds according to the crochet diagram. Work Round 1 around an adjustable foundation ring (= magic loop). For a neat transition change the color before the slip stitch at the end of the round. If the symbols meet at the bottom, insert the hook into the same stitch.

Front and back post double crochet: For front and back post double crochet, don't insert the hook into the stitch of the previous row or round, but guide it around the vertical loop of the lower stitch. Inserting the hook from front to back creates a front post double crochet; inserting the hook from back to front creates a back post double crochet.

Rib pattern in rounds (uneven number of stitches): Round 1: 1 turning chain (it doesn't replace any stitch), work single crochets, close the round with 1 slip stitch into the 1st single crochet. Round 2: 3 turning chains (to replace the 1st double crochet), work double crochets, close the round with 1 slip stitch in the topmost 1st turning chain. Round 3: 2 turning chains (to replace the 1st front post double crochet), * 1 front post double crochet, 1 back post double crochet, keep repeating from *, 1 front post double crochet, close the round with 1 slip stitch in the topmost 1st turning chain. Work Rounds 1–3 1x, then keep repeating Round 3.

Picot: 3 chain stitches, 1 single crochet into the 1st chain stitch

Color sequence A: 2 rounds blue, 1 round light blue, 2 rounds beige

Color sequence B: 2 rounds cyan, 1 round mint, 2 rounds beige

Color sequence C: 2 rounds fir green, 1 round linden green, 2 rounds beige

Color sequence D: 2 rounds moss, 1 round green, 2 rounds beige

Color sequence E: 2 rounds dusky pink, 1 round pink, 2 rounds beige

Color sequence F: 2 rounds bordeaux, 1 round cyclamen, 2 rounds beige

Color sequence G: 2 rounds red, 1 round raspberry, 2 rounds beige

Color sequence H: 2 rounds terracotta, 1 round apricot, 2 rounds beige

INSTRUCTIONS

Crochet 2 squares each over 5 rounds in each color sequence.

Eye (32x): Work around an adjustable foundation ring in natural. Round 1: 6 single crochets.

Round 2: 2 single crochets into 1 stitch = 12 single crochets. Finish the work.

TIP To avoid having to fasten off the tails, let them run along the back while crocheting, and crochet around them.

ASSEMBLY

For the ears, crochet in the front free loops of Round 3 of the squares in the color of Round 3 as follows: chain, 1 slip stitch, 1 single crochet, 1 half double crochet, (2 double crochets, 1 picot, 2 double crochets) in 1 stitch, 1 half double crochet, 1 single crochet, 3 slip stitches, 1 single crochet, 1 half double crochet, (2 double crochets, 1 picot, 2 double crochets) in 1 stitch, 1 half double crochet, 1 single crochet, 1 slip stitch. Finish the work. Stitch a knot stitch each in black in the center of the eyes. Sew 2 eyes each onto each owl. Stitch the beaks and feet in yellow (see photo). According to the cut, crochet the squares together in beige, working slip stitches from the right. For the facing crochet 4 rounds in rib pattern in beige around the neckline. For the cuffs, work another 8 rounds in rib pattern in beige over 3.3 in each on both sides of the shoulder seam. Crochet 1 round reverse single crochets (= single crochets from left to right) in beige around the bottom edge of the poncho.

Crochet diagram

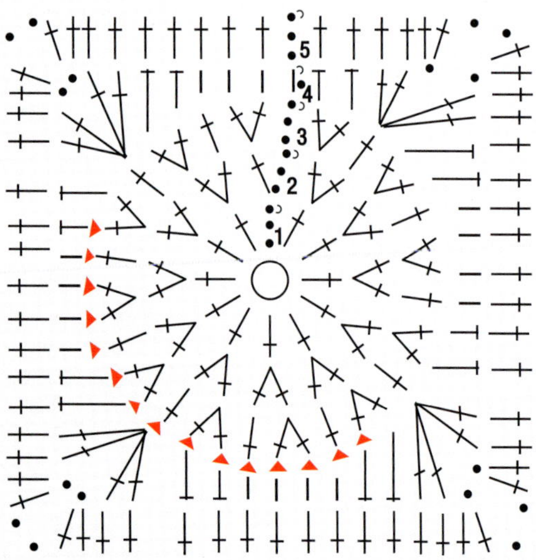

Key

- • = 1 chain stitch
- c = 1 slip stitch
- | = 1 single crochet
- T = 1 half double crochet
- † = 1 double crochet
- ▼ = Only work into the back loop.

If the symbols meet at the bottom, insert the hook into the same stitch. If the symbols meet at the top, decrease the stitches together.

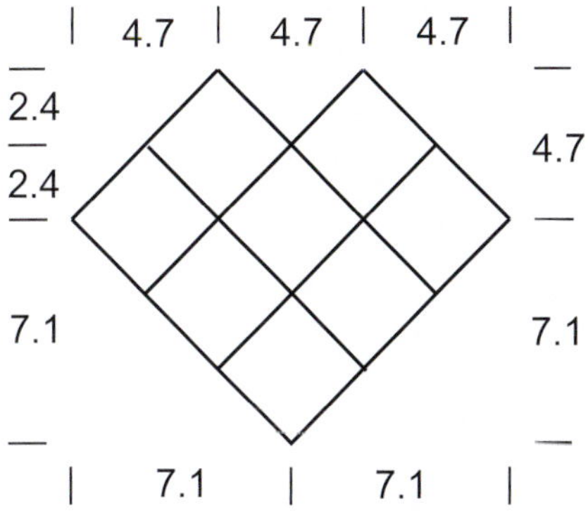
4.7
4.7
4.7
2.4
2.4
4.7
7.1
7.1
7.1
7.1

BELLA BABY CAP

SIZE

1–2 months, 3–9 months, and 9–18 months
The specifications for the larger sizes are in parentheses. If there is only one specification, it applies to all sizes.

MATERIALS

Cap shown worked in **ONline Linie 110 Timona**** (60% pure wool, 40% acrylic, 131 yd / 1.8 oz) using the following colors and amounts:
23 Ecru: 1.8 oz
35 Taupe: 1.8 oz
46 Purple: 1.8 oz
**If you have trouble finding this yarn, see the Conversion Chart on page 126 for substitutions.

Crochet hook G-6

GAUGE

1 square over 7 rounds = 4.7 in x 4.7 in

PATTERN

Crochet square: Work 13 (14 / 15) rounds according to the crochet diagram on p 21. Work Round 1 around an adjustable foundation ring (= magic loop). For a neat transition change the color before decreasing the half double crochet at the end of the round. Close the last round as shown for Round 5 in the diagram.

Single crochets: Begin each round with 1 turning chain (it doesn't replace any stitch), and close the round with 1 slip stitch in the 1st single crochet.

Color sequence: * 1 round ecru, 1 round taupe, 1 round purple, repeat from *.

INSTRUCTIONS

Crochet 2 squares over 12 (13 / 14) rounds in the color sequence.

ASSEMBLY

Close the back and top seams: crochet together the squares, working slip stitches in ecru from the right side. Crochet 1 round single crochets in ecru around the bottom and face edges. Then crochet 1 round each of single crochets in taupe and lilac around those edges, working 1 chain of 40 (50 / 60) chain stitches in each corner in Round 1, and crochet these back with single crochets. Crochet these with single crochets as well in Round 2.

TIP To avoid having to fasten off the tails, let them run along the back while crocheting, and crochet around them.

BOTTLE HOLDER

SIZE

For a bottle with a circumference of approx 9 in

MATERIALS

Bottle Holder shown worked in **Schoeller + Stahl Limone**** (100% cotton, 137 yd / 1.8 oz) using the following colors and amounts:
14 May Green: 1.8 oz
21 Polar Blue: 1.8 oz
73 Natural: 1.8 oz
192 Gold: 1.8 oz
**If you have trouble finding this yarn, see the Conversion Chart on page 126 for substitutions.

Crochet hook D

GAUGE

1 square over 4 rounds = 3 in x 3 in

PATTERN

Crochet square: Work 4 rounds according to the crochet diagram. Work Round 1 around an adjustable foundation ring (= magic loop). For a neat transition change the color before the slip stitch at the end of the round. Work Rounds 1–4 1x.

Single crochets: Begin each round with 1 turning chain (it doesn't replace any stitch), and close the round with 1 slip stitch in the 1st single crochet.

Color sequence A: 1 round gold, 1 round natural, 2 rounds May green

Color sequence B: 1 round gold, 1 round natural, 2 rounds polar blue

INSTRUCTIONS

Body: Crochet 3 squares each in color sequences A and B over 4 rounds.

Bottom: Work around an adjustable foundation ring, crocheting 8 single crochets in polar blue around the ring. To give it shape, increase 9 single crochets, each evenly distributed 6x in each round, working 2 single crochets each in 1 stitch = 56 single crochets.

Straps: Chain 151 chain stitches + 3 turning chains (to replace the 1st double crochet) in May green. Row 1: 3 turning chains (to replace the 1st double crochet), * skip 2 chains, 3 double crochets in 1 chain, keep repeating from *, skip 2 chains, 1 double crochet. Finish the work. Row 2: Work this row on the other side of the chain stitches: 3 turning chains (to replace the 1st double crochet), 1 double crochet in the same stitch, 3 double crochets each around each gap of the 1st row, 2 double crochet in the last double crochet. Finish the work.

ASSEMBLY

Crochet 3 squares each together, working slip stitches in the respective color from the right and closing them to a ring. Crochet the two rings together, working slip stitches in polar blue from the right side. Crochet the bottom and the bottom ring together, working single crochets from the right side. Crochet 1 round single crochets in May green around the top edge of the body. Sew the straps to the top edge of the body.

Crochet diagram

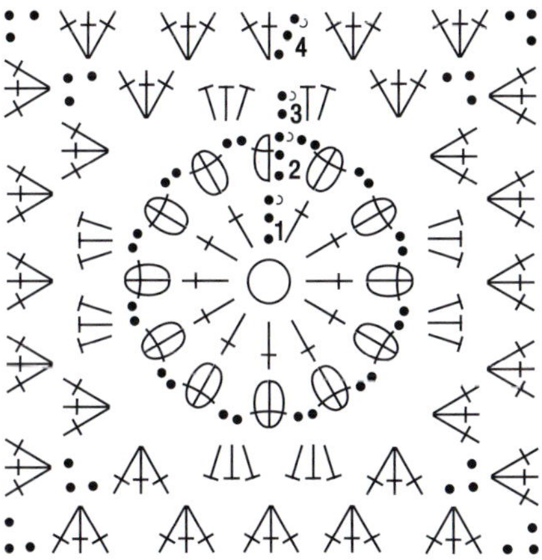

Key

- • = 1 chain stitch
- c = 1 single crochet
- T = 1 half double crochet
- † = 1 double crochet
- ∀ = 2 double crochets together
- ⊕ = 3 double crochets together

If the symbols meet at the bottom, insert the hook into the same stitch. If the symbols meet at the top, decrease the stitches together.

SLEEPING BAG

SIZE

16 in x 32 in

MATERIALS

Sleeping Bag shown worked in **Buttinette Woll Butt Primo Madeleine**** (100% pure wool, 164 yd / 1.8 oz) using the following colors and amounts:
102.911 Sage: 5 oz
103.823 Light Gray: 3.5 oz
142.30 Wool White: 1.8 oz
229.93 Taupe: 3.5 oz
253.47 Dark Gray: 5 oz
**If you have trouble finding this yarn, see the Conversion Chart on page 125 for substitutions.

Crochet hook D

GAUGE

1 square over 6 rounds = 4 in x 4 in

PATTERN

Crochet square: Work 6 rounds according to the crochet diagram on p 21. Work Round 1 around an adjustable foundation ring (= magic loop). For a neat transition change the color before decreasing the half double crochet at the end of the round. Close the last round as shown for Round 5 in the diagram.

Single crochets: Begin each row with 1 turning chain (it doesn't replace any stitch). Begin each round with 1 turning chain (it doesn't replace any stitch), and close the round with 1 slip stitch in the 1st single crochet.

Color sequence A: * 1 round wool white, 2 rounds taupe, 3 rounds sage, keep repeating from *.

Color sequence B: * 1 round wool white, 2 rounds light gray, 3 rounds dark gray, keep repeating from *.

INSTRUCTIONS

Front: Crochet 10 squares each over 6 rounds in color sequences A and B.

Back and hood: Crochet 16 squares over 6 rounds in color sequences A and B.

ASSEMBLY

Crochet the squares together according to the diagram, working slip stitches in sage from the right side. Crochet 1 row single crochet in sage around the top edge of the front. For the top hood seams fold the top corners of the back together (= 8 in), and crochet together with 1 row single crochet in sage. Crochet together the front and back as well as around the face edge of the hood, working 1 round single crochet in sage.

TIP To avoid having to fasten off the tails, let them run along the back while crocheting, and crochet around them.

Diagram

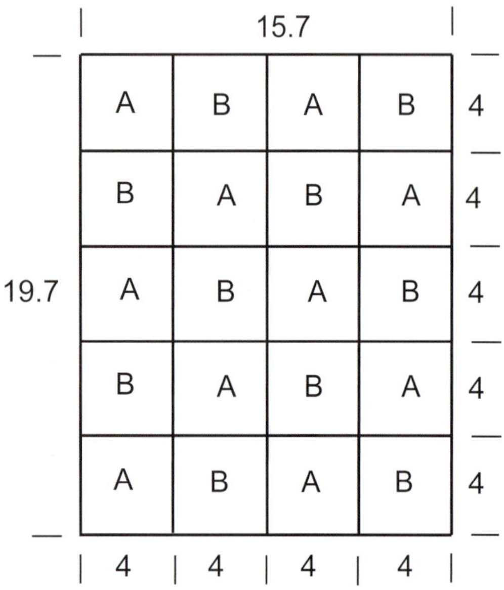
15.7
19.7
A B A B 4
B A B A 4
A B A B 4
B A B A 4
A B A B 4
4 4 4 4

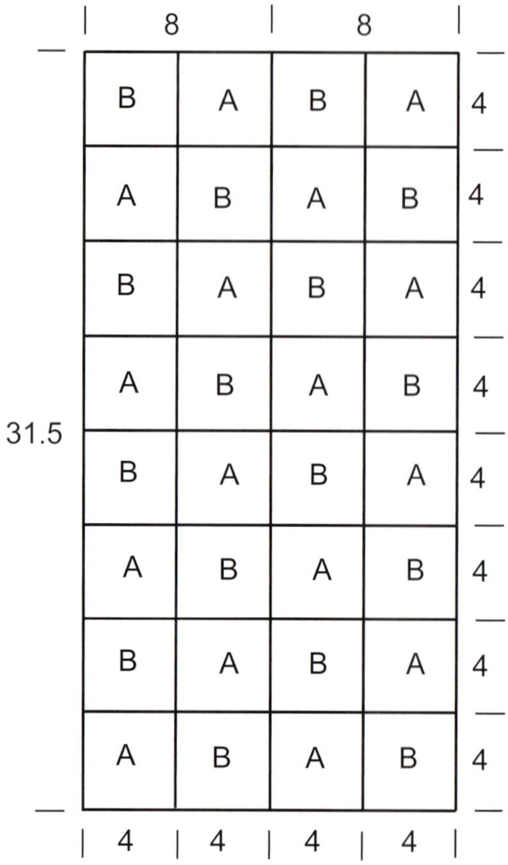
8 8
31.5
B A B A 4
A B A B 4
B A B A 4
A B A B 4
B A B A 4
A B A B 4
B A B A 4
A B A B 4
4 4 4 4

COZY BLANKET

SIZE

22 in x 22 in

MATERIALS

Blanket shown worked in **Lana Grossa Cool Wool Vintage**** (100% pure wool, 175 yd / 1.8 oz) using the following colors and amounts:

7361 Olive: 1.8 oz	7362 Mustard: 1.8 oz
7365 Plum: 1.8 oz	7366 Dark Blue: 1.8 oz
7369 Light Gray: 3.5 oz	7370 Anthracite: 3.5 oz
7372 Violet: 1.8 oz	

**If you have trouble finding this yarn, see the Conversion Chart on page 126 for substitutions.

Crochet hook D

GAUGE

1 square over 7 rounds = 3.5 in x 3.5 in

PATTERN

Crochet square: Work 7 rounds according to the crochet diagram on p 21. Work Round 1 around an adjustable foundation ring (= magic loop). For a neat transition change the color before decreasing the half double crochet at the end of the round. Close the last round as shown for Round 5 in the diagram.

Double crochet pattern in rounds: Round 1: 3 turning chains (to replace the 1st double crochet), 1 double crochet in the same stitch, * 3 double crochets between the 3 double crochets of the previous round, keep repeating from *, 1 double crochet in the same stitch as the 1st double crochet, close the round with 1 slip stitch in the topmost turning chain. Round 2: 3 turning chains (to replace the 1st double crochet), * 3 double crochets between the 3 double crochets of the previous round, keep repeating from *, close the round with 1 slip stitch in the topmost turning chain. Keep repeating Rounds 1 and 2.

Color sequence A: * 1 round anthracite, 1 round mustard, 1 round violet, keep repeating from *.

Color sequence B: * 1 round olive, 1 round plum, 1 round dark blue, work 2x from *, 1 round light gray

Color sequence C: 1 round anthracite, 1 round olive, 1 round light gray, 1 round dark blue, 1 round plum, 1 round mustard, and 1 round anthracite

INSTRUCTIONS

Crochet 13 squares over 7 rounds in color sequence A, and 12 squares over 7 rounds in color sequence B.

ASSEMBLY

Crochet the squares together in anthracite according to the diagram, working slip stitches from the right side. Keep inserting the hook into the back loops of both squares, and pull the thread through from the back. Crochet 7 rounds double crochet in color sequence C, working the corners as shown in the crochet diagram.

TIP To avoid having to fasten off the tails, let them run along the back while crocheting, and crochet around them.

Diagram

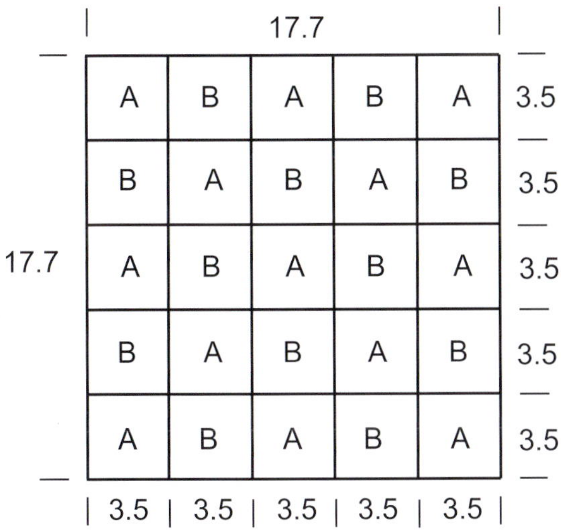
17.7
A B A B A
B A B A B
A B A B A
B A B A B
A B A B A
17.7
3.5 3.5 3.5 3.5 3.5
3.5 3.5 3.5 3.5 3.5

BONZO BUNNY

SIZE

Height: 18.5 in

MATERIALS

Bonzo Bunny shown worked in **Lang Yarns Venus**** (50% pure wool, 50% cotton, 186 yd / 1.8 oz) using the following colors and amounts:
0009 Pink: 1.8 oz
0040 Ice Blue: 1.8 oz
0044 Lime: 1.8 oz
0047 Purple: 1.8 oz
0066 Red: 1.8 oz
0074 Petrol Green: 1.8 oz
0077 Terracotta: 1.8 oz
**If you have trouble finding this yarn, see the Conversion Chart on page 126 for substitutions.

Crochet hook G-6
Polyester fiberfill

GAUGE

1 square over 6 rounds = 4 in x 4 in
16.5 single crochets over 19 rounds = 4 in x 4 in

Note: Work the square with one yarn and the other parts of the bunny with two yarns.

PATTERN

Crochet square: Work 6 rounds according to the crochet diagram on p 21. Work Round 1 around an adjustable foundation ring (= magic loop). For a neat transition change the color before decreasing the half double crochet at the end of the round. Close the last round as shown for Round 5 in the diagram.

Single crochet: Begin each round with 1 turning chain (it doesn't replace any stitch), and close the round with 1 slip stitch in the 1st single crochet.

INSTRUCTIONS

Belly: Crochet 1 square over 9 rounds, working 1 round each in pink, ice blue, terracotta, petrol green, red, and purple. Then crochet 1 round reverse single crochet (= single crochets from left to right) in lime.

TIP To avoid having to fasten off the tails, let them run along the back while crocheting, and crochet around them.

Left leg: Work with two yarns in terracotta around an adjustable foundation ring. Round 1: 8 single crochets. Round 2: Keep working 2 single crochets in 1 stitch = 16 single crochets. Round 3: * 1 single crochet, 2 single crochets in 1 stitch, work 8x from * = 24 single crochets. Round 4: 24 back loop single crochets. Rounds 5–7: 24 single crochets. Round 8, lime: 24 single crochets. Rounds 9–27: 24 single crochets. Finish the work. Stuff the leg with fiberfill.

Right leg: Work with two yarns in petrol green around an adjustable foundation ring. Round 1: 8 single crochets. Round 2: Keep working 2 single crochets in 1 stitch = 16 single crochets. Round 3: * 1 single crochet, 2 single crochets in 1 stitch, work 8x from * = 24 single crochets. Round 4: 24 back loop single crochets. Rounds 5–12: 24 single crochets. Rounds 13–16: 24 single crochets. Round 17–27, red: 24 single crochets. Stuff the leg with fiberfill.

Body, head, and ears: Continue working single crochets with two yarns in ice blue over the stitches of both legs, working the first 6 single crochets in the 1st round in both legs = 36 single crochets. To give it shape, increase 6 stitches each 1x in the 1st round and 1x in the following 2nd round, working 2 single crochets each 6x in 1 stitch = 48 single crochets. Stuff with fiberfill. Decrease 6 stitches after 22 rounds from the beginning of the body, working 2 single crochets each evenly distributed 6x together = 42 single crochets. Once you've used up the ice blue yarn, continue working in pink. Stuff with fiberfill. After 43 rounds from the beginning of the body, crochet the 2 stitches before the end of the round to 2 stitches after the beginning of the round together with the opposite 4 stitches, so that 17 stitches each remain left and right per ear.

Left ear: Rounds 1–9, pink: 17 single crochets. Round 10: Decrease 2 single crochets together, 6 single crochets, decrease 2 single crochets together, 7 single crochets = 15 single crochets. Rounds 11–13: 15 single crochets. Stuff with fiberfill. Round 14, purple: Decrease 2 single crochets together, 5 single crochets, decrease 2 single crochets together, 6 single crochets = 13 single crochets. Round 15, lime: 13 single crochets. Round 16: Decrease 2 single crochets together, 4 single crochets, decrease 2 single crochets together, 5 single crochets = 11 single crochets. Keep decreasing 2 single crochets together until there are no stitches left. Finish the work.

Right ear: Rounds 1–5: 17 single crochets. Rounds 6–9, terracotta: 17 single crochets. Round 10: Decrease 2 single crochets together, 6 single crochets, decrease 2 single crochets together, 7 single crochets = 15 single crochets. Rounds 11–13: 15 single crochets. Stuff with fiberfill. Round 14: Decrease 2 single crochets together, 5 single crochets, decrease 2 single crochets together, 6 single crochets = 13 single crochets. Round 15: 13 single crochets. Round 16, petrol green: Decrease 2 single crochets together, 4 single crochets, decrease 2 single crochets together, 5 single crochets = 11 single crochets. Keep decreasing 2 single crochets together until there are no stitches left. Finish the work.

Left arm: Work with two yarns in terracotta around an adjustable foundation ring. Round 1: 8 single crochets. Round 2: Keep working 2 single crochets in 1 stitch = 16 single crochets. Round 3: 16 single crochets only in the back loop. Rounds 4–6: 16 single crochets. Round 7, lime: 16 single crochets. Round 8–27, red: 16 single crochets. Stuff with fiberfill. Fold over the work, and crochet together the top edge with 1 row 8 single crochets. Finish the work.

Right arm: Work with two yarns in petrol green around an adjustable foundation ring. Round 1: 8 single crochets. Round 2: Keep working 2 single crochets in 1 stitch = 16 single crochets. Round 3: 16 single crochets in the back loop only. Rounds 4–7: 16 single crochets. Round 8–13, purple: 16 single crochets. Rounds 14–27, red: 16 single crochets. Stuff with fiberfill. Fold over the work, and crochet together the top edge with 1 row 8 single crochets. Finish the work.

Left eye: Work with two yarns in terracotta around an adjustable foundation ring. Round 1: 6 single crochets. Round 2, petrol green: Keep working 2 single crochets in 1 stitch = 12 single crochets. Round 3: * 1 single crochet, 2 single crochets in 1 stitch, work 6x = 18 single crochets from *. Round 4, purple: * 2 single crochets, 2 single crochets in 1 stitch, work 6x = 24 single crochets from *. Finish the work.

Right eye: Work with two yarns in lime around an adjustable foundation ring. Round 1: 6 single crochets. Round 2, purple: Keep working 2 single crochets in 1 stitch = 12 single crochets. Round 3: * 1 single crochet, 2 single crochets in 1 stitch, work 6x = 18 single crochets from *. Round 4, red: * 2 single crochets, 2 single crochets in 1 stitch, work 6x = 24 single crochets from *. Finish the work.

Snout: Work with two yarns in pink around an adjustable foundation ring. Round 1: 6 single crochets. Finish the work.

Tail: Work with two yarns in terracotta around an adjustable foundation ring. Round 1: 6 single crochets. Round 2: Keep working 2 single crochets in 1 stitch = 12 single crochets. Round 3, petrol green: * 1 single crochet, 2 single crochet into 1 stitch, work 6x = 18 single crochets from *. Round 4: * 2 single crochets, 2 single crochets in 1 stitch, work 6x = 24 single crochets from *. Rounds 5 and 6: 24 single crochets. Finish the work.

ASSEMBLY

Sew the arms onto the sides of the body. Stuff the tail with fiberfill, and sew it onto the lower back. Sew the square onto the belly. Sew the eyes and the snout onto the head. Stitch on the whiskers with one yarn in terracotta (see photo). Sew on the left ear at an angle.

ANIMAL BLOCK

SIZE

3.2 in x 3.2 in

MATERIALS

Block shown worked in **Buttinette Woll Butt Camilla**** (100% cotton, 137 yd / 1.8 oz) using the following colors and amounts:

102.688 Fir: 1.8 oz	103.767 Beige: 1.8 oz
103.768 Navy Blue: 1.8 oz	103.769 Natural: 1.8 oz
115.78 Lobster Red: 1.8 oz	142.56 Powder: 1.8 oz
218.77 Chocolate: 1.8 oz	240.39 Aqua: 1.8 oz
271.55 Dark Gray: 1.8 oz	354.32 White: 1.8 oz
354. 35 Black: 1.8 oz	354.36 Vanilla: 1.8 oz
354.43 Orange: 1.8 oz	359.33 Green: 1.8 oz
359.80 Bordeaux: 1.8 oz	

**If you have trouble finding this yarn, see the Conversion Chart on page 125 for substitutions.

Crochet hook D

Polyester fiberfill or a foam cube with an edge length of 3.2 in

GAUGE

1 square over 5 rounds = 3.2 in x 3.2 in

PATTERN

Crochet square: Work 5 rounds according to the crochet diagram. Work Round 1 around an adjustable foundation ring (= magic loop). For a neat transition change the color before the slip stitch at the end of the round. If the symbols meet at the bottom, insert the hook into the same stitch.

Picot: 3 chain stitches, 1 slip stitch into the 1st chain stitch.

INSTRUCTIONS

TIP To avoid having to fasten off the tails, let them run along the back while crocheting, and crochet around them.

Frog: Crochet 1 square over 5 rounds, working 3 rounds in green and 2 rounds in bordeaux.
Eye (2x): Work in white around an adjustable foundation ring. Round 1: 6 single crochets. Round 2: 2 single crochets each in 1 stitch = 12 single crochets. Round 3, green: 12 slip stitches around the front loops. Round 4: 12 slip stitches around the back loops of the 3rd round. Finish the work.
Assemble the Frog: Stitch a knot stitch each in black in the center of the eyes. Sew on the eyes. For the mouth, stitch a stem stitch in black.

Fox: Crochet 1 square over 5 rounds, working 3 rounds in orange and 2 rounds in terracotta.
Snout: Work in white around an adjustable foundation ring. Round 1: 6 single crochets. Finish the work.
Lower half of the face: Work in white around an adjustable foundation ring. Round 1: 12 double crochets. Round 2: 4 chain stitches, 1 treble crochet in the same stitch, 2 double crochets in 1 stitch, 2 half double stitches in 1 stitch, 2 single crochets each 2x in 1 stitch, 2 half double crochets in 1 stitch, 2 double crochets in 1 stitch,

2 treble crochets in 1 stitch, leave the remaining stitches as they are. Finish the work.

Ear (2x): Chain 8 chain stitches in orange. Row 1: Starting at the 4th stitch from the hook, decrease 4 treble crochets together, 1 chain. Cut off the thread. Row 2: Starting in the bottom right corner of the 1st row, work 3 single crochets in white in the side edge, 1 picot, 3 single crochets in the other side edge. Finish the work.
Assemble the Fox: Sew the snout onto the lower half of the face. Sew on the ears. For the eyes stitch 1 knot stitch each in black.

Piglet: Crochet 1 square over 5 rounds, working 3 rounds in powder and 2 rounds in navy blue.
Snout: Work around an adjustable foundation ring in lobster red. Round 1: 6 single crochets. Round 2, powder: 2 single crochets each in 1 stitch = 12 single crochets. Round 3: 12 slip stitches. Finish the work.
Ear (2x): Work around an adjustable foundation ring in lobster red. Row 1: 2 single crochets, 1 half double crochet, 1 double crochet, 1 half double crochet, 2 single crochets. Row 2, powder: 3 single crochets, (1 single crochet, 1 picot, 1 single crochet) in 1 stitch, 3 single crochets, slip stitches to the beginning of the row, close the round with 1 single crochet. Finish the work.
Assemble the Piglet: Stitch two nostrils in black on the snout, using puff stitches. Sew on the snout. Sew on the ear. For the eyes stitch 1 knot stitch each in black.

Rabbit: Crochet 1 square over 5 rounds, working 3 rounds in natural and 2 rounds in lobster red.
Snout: Chain 6 chain stitches in chocolate. Row 1: Decrease 2 double crochets together from the 3rd stitch from the hook. Finish the work.
Cheek (2x): Work in beige around an adjustable foundation ring. Round 1: 6 single crochets. Finish the work.
Ear (2x): Chain 5 chain stitches in beige. Round 1: 3 single crochets, (2 half double crochets, 1 double crochet, 2 half double crochets) in 1 stitch, keep working on the other side of the chains, 3 single crochets. Round 2, natural: 2 slip stitches, 2 single crochets, 2 half double crochets in 1 stitch, (1 double crochet, 1 picot, 1 double crochet) in 1 stitch, 2 half double crochets in 1 stitch, 2 single crochets, 2 slip stitches. Finish the work.
Assemble the Rabbit: Sew on the snout and 1 cheek each on both sides. Stitch the mouth in chocolate (see photo). Sew on the ears. For the eyes stitch 1 knot stitch each in black.

Chicken: Crochet 1 square over 5 rounds, working 3 rounds in vanilla and 2 rounds in dark gray.
Beak: Chain 6 chain stitches in orange. Row 1: Decrease 3 double crochets together from the 3rd stitch from the hook. Finish the work.
Comb: * Chain 4 chain stitches in bordeaux, and work 3 slip stitches from the 2nd stitch from the hook, work 3x from *. Finish the work.
Assemble the Chicken: Sew on the beak in the center. Stitch the eyes in puff stitches in black. Sew on the comb.

Sheep: Crochet 1 square over 5 rounds, working 3 rounds in natural and 2 rounds in aqua. Insert the hook in the back loops only in the 1st round.
Hair: Work around an adjustable foundation ring in natural. Round 1: 12 double crochets. Round 2: 1 chain stitch, * skip 1 stitch, 5 double crochets in 1 stitch, skip 1 stitch, 1 slip stitch, work 2x from *. Finish the work.
Head: Work around an adjustable foundation ring in chocolate. Round 1: 12 double crochets. Round 2: 2 single crochets each in 1 stitch = 24 single crochets. Finish the work.
Ear (2x): Chain 5 chain stitches in chocolate. Finish the work.
Assemble the Sheep: Crochet 1 round in natural in the free loops of the 3rd round as follows:

chain 1 chain stitch, * 1 slip stitch, skip 1 stitch, 5 double crochets in 1 stitch, keep repeating from *, and close the round with 1 slip stitch. Sew on the head, and sew on the ears on both sides. Sew on the hair. Stitch the eyes in white. Stitch the pupils with knot stitches in black.

ASSEMBLY

Crochet the squares together from the right side in the desired color sequence, working in the back loops. Stuff with fiberfill or the foam cube before closing the last side seam.

TIP For a more distinct die shape, sew an 8 in x 8 in cube from fabric, and stuff with fiberfill.

Crochet diagram

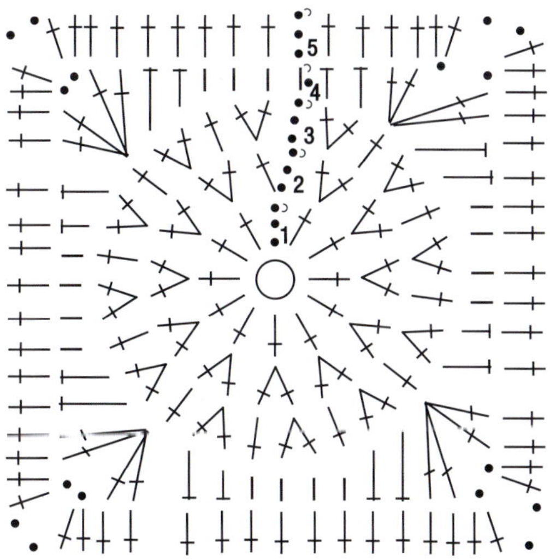

Key

- • = 1 chain stitch
- c = 1 slip stitch
- | = 1 single crochet
- T = 1 half double crochet
- † = 1 double crochet

If the symbols meet at the bottom, insert the hook into the same stitch. If the symbols meet at the top, decrease the stitches together.

HOT-WATER BOTTLE COVER

SIZE

7 in x 7 in

MATERIALS

Cover shown worked in **Austermann Merino 160**** (100% pure wool, 175 yd / 1.8 oz) using the following colors and amounts:

228 Light Gray: 1.8 oz
233 Petrol Blue: 1.8 oz
235 Turquoise: 1.8 oz
241 Pink Lipstick: 1.8 oz
256 Lollipop: 1.8 oz
259 Mint: 1.8 oz
261 Azalea: 1.8 oz
266 Powder: 1.8 oz
273 Grass Green: 1.8 oz

**If you have trouble finding this yarn, see the Conversion Chart on page 125 for substitutions.

Crochet hook D
Baby hot-water bottle, 7 in x 7 in

GAUGE

1 square over 3 rounds = 2 in x 2 in

PATTERN

Crochet square: Work 3 rounds according to the crochet diagram on p 21. Work Round 1 around an adjustable foundation ring (= magic loop). For a neat transition change the color before decreasing the half double crochet at the end of the round. Close the last round as shown for Round 5 in the diagram.

Single crochets: Begin each round with 1 turning chain (it doesn't replace any stitch), and close the round with 1 slip stitch in the 1st single crochet.

Front and back post double crochet: For front and back post double crochet, don't insert the hook into the stitch of the previous row or round, but guide it around the vertical loop of the lower stitch. Inserting the hook from front to back creates a front post double crochet; inserting the hook from back to front creates a back post double crochet.

Rip pattern in rounds (uneven number of stitches): Round 1: 1 turning chain (it doesn't replace any stitch), work single crochets, close the round with 1 slip stitch in the 1st single crochet. Round 2: 3 turning chains (to replace the 1st double crochet), work double crochets, close the round with 1 slip stitch in the topmost turning chain. Round 3: 2 turning chains (to replace the 1st double crochet), * 1 front post double crochet, 1 back post double crochet, keep repeating from *, close the round with 1 slip stitch in the topmost turning chain. Work Rounds 1 and 3 1x, then keep repeating Round 3.

INSTRUCTIONS

Side 1: Crochet 9 squares over 3 rounds in the desired color sequence in pink shades.

Side 2: Crochet 9 squares over 3 rounds in the desired color sequence in blue-green shades.

ASSEMBY

Crochet 9 squares each in pink or blue-green shades together, working slip stitches from the right side in light gray. Crochet 3 rounds each single crochets in light gray around the outer edge of both sides, working 3 single crochets each in the corners in each round.
For the bottleneck crochet 14 rounds in rib pattern in light gray = 40 stitches over the middle 20 stitches of the top edge of both sides, increasing 1 stitch in the 1st round = 41 stitches. Next, crochet together the outer edge of both sides, working 1 row single crochets in light gray and inserting the hot-water bottle.

Note: If you like, leave the bottom edge open, and either sew in a zipper (made from plastic, for it won't get warm) or sew on buttons and button loops.

Note: For a hot-water bottle in pink or blue-green shades only, crochet 18 squares over 3 rounds in the desired color sequence. You can also work the squares with leftover yarn.

TIP To avoid having to fasten off the tails, let them run along the back while crocheting, and crochet around them.

CROCHET: THE STITCHES

ADJUSTABLE FOUNDATION RING (= MAGIC LOOP)

1 Form a loop with the yarn, insert the crochet hook, place the thread around the hook, and pull the yarn over through. Don't pull the foundation ring tight yet. Place the working thread around your left index finger.

2 Hold the crosspoint of the foundation ring with your thumb and middle finger, work a yarn over, and pull it through the ring on the hook.

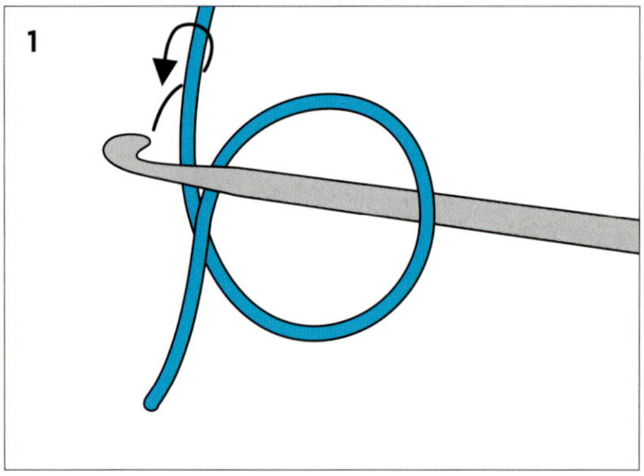

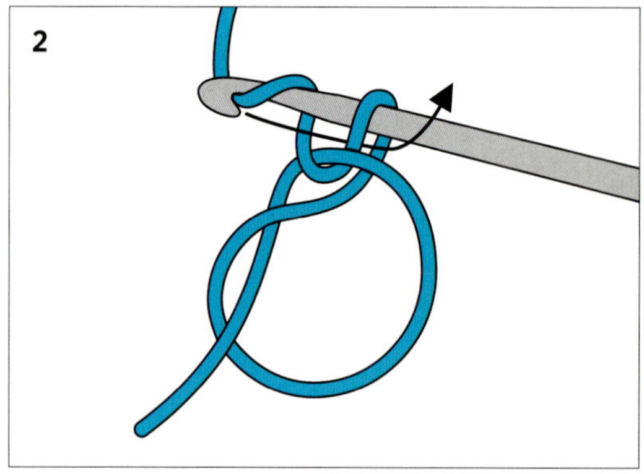

3 Work the stitches around the foundation ring according to the instructions. Close the round with a slip stitch, and pull the foundation ring tight at the beginning. (Below: single crochets)

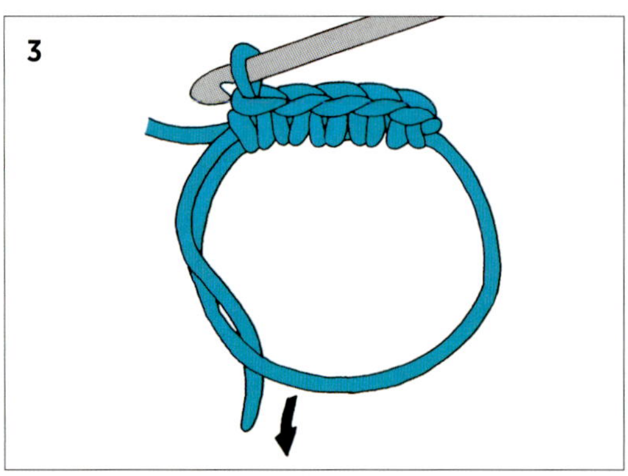

CHAIN STITCH

Insert the hook in the loop, and place the yarn around your index finger over the hook from back to front (= yarn over). Pull the yarn through the loop.

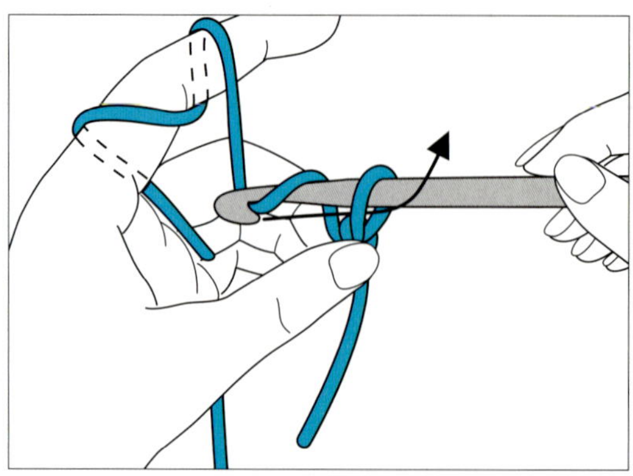

SINGLE CROCHET

1 Insert the hook in both loops of the stitch, and yarn over (= place it around the hook from back to front). Pull this yarn over through the loops.

2 There are now two loops on the hook. Yarn over again, and pull it through both loops on the hook. This last step that completes a stitch is called "decreasing."

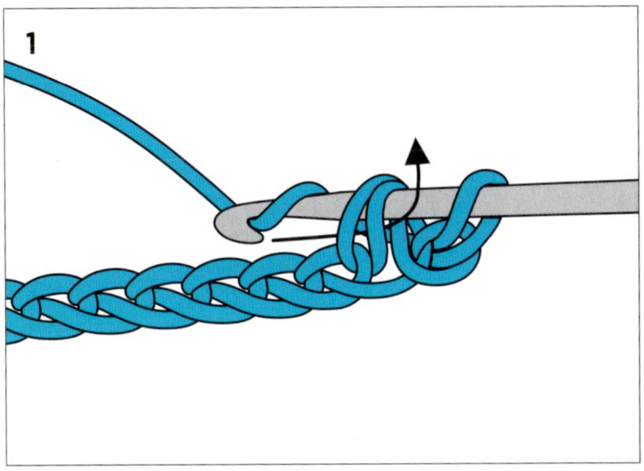

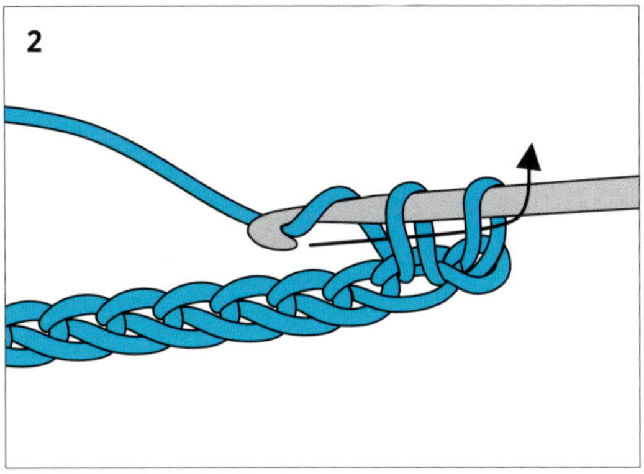

SLIP STITCH

Insert the hook in both loops of the stitch, and yarn over. Pull this yarn over straight through the stitch and the loop on the hook.

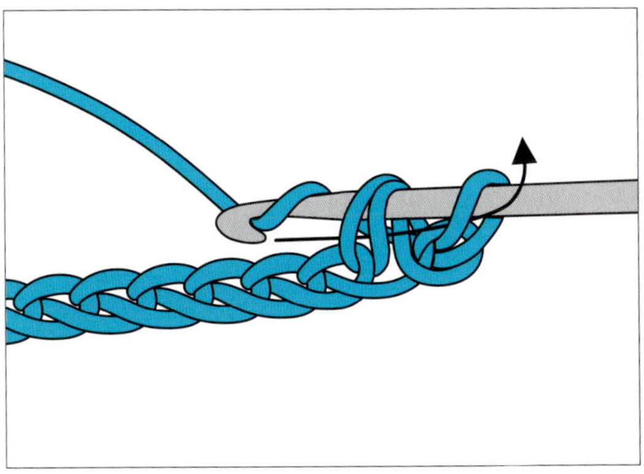

SINGLE CROCHETS IN ROUNDS

Close the round with 1 single crochet in the 1st stitch, and pull the foundation ring tight at the beginning. Begin each round with 1 additional turning chain, and close the round with 1 slip stitch in the 1st single crochet.

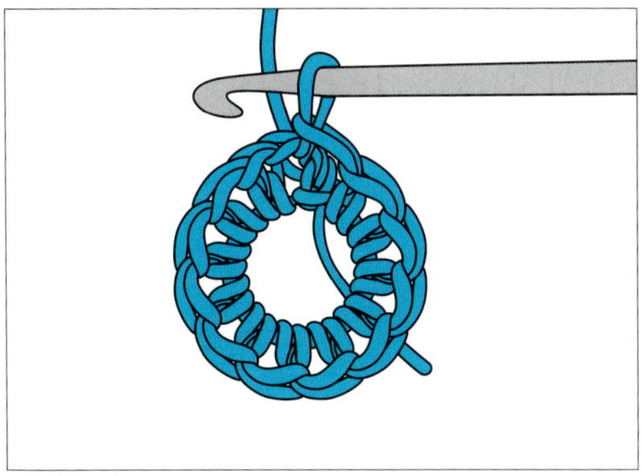

SINGLE CROCHETS IN SPIRALS

To begin, chain the specified number of chain stitches. Don't close the round with a slip stitch, but insert the hook directly into the 1st stitch of the previous round. Mark the first stitch of each new round with a different-colored yarn, or use a stitch marker.

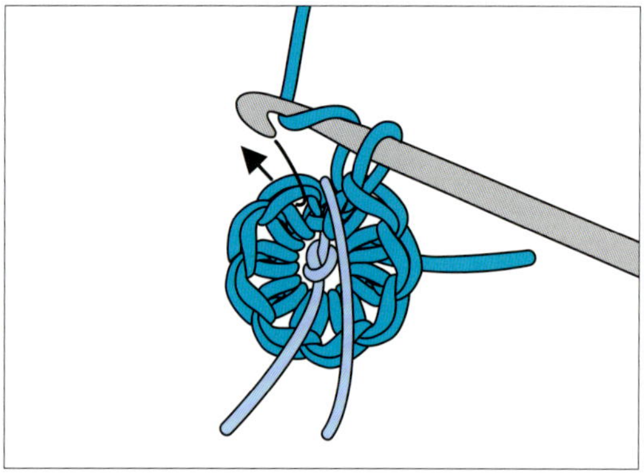

HALF DOUBLE CROCHET

1 Pull the yarn from back to front around the hook, and insert the hook in both loops of the stitch. Yarn over and pull it through the stitches.

2 As with a double crochet, there are now 3 loops on the hook. Work another yarn over, and decrease all 3 loops on the hook together.

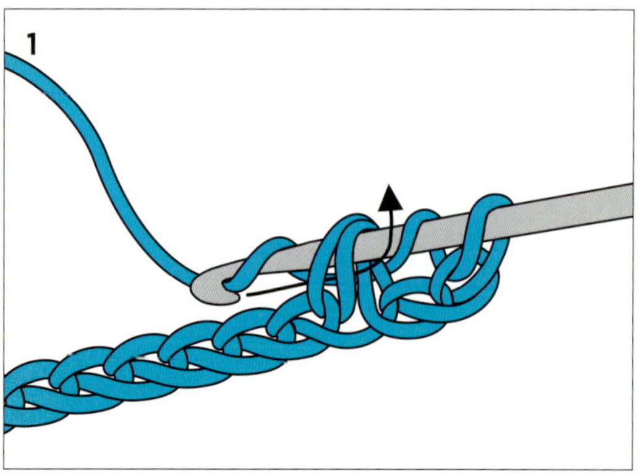

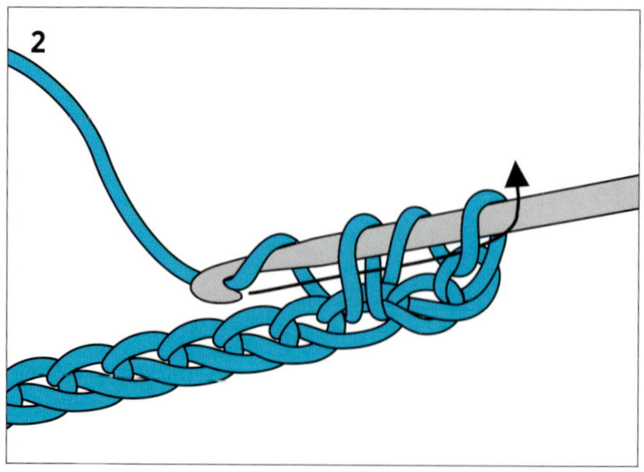

DOUBLE CROCHET

1 The 1st double crochet of the row is replaced by 3 chain stitches. Make a loop, yarn over, and insert the hook in the 4th stitch off the hook, pulling the yarn through the stitch.

2 Yarn over again, and only pull through 2 of the 3 loops on the hook.

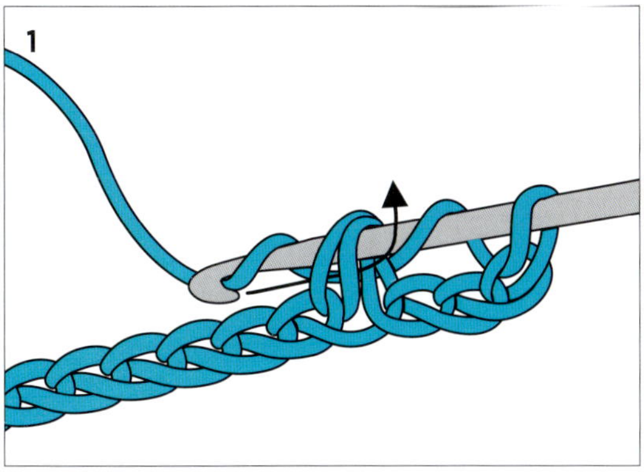

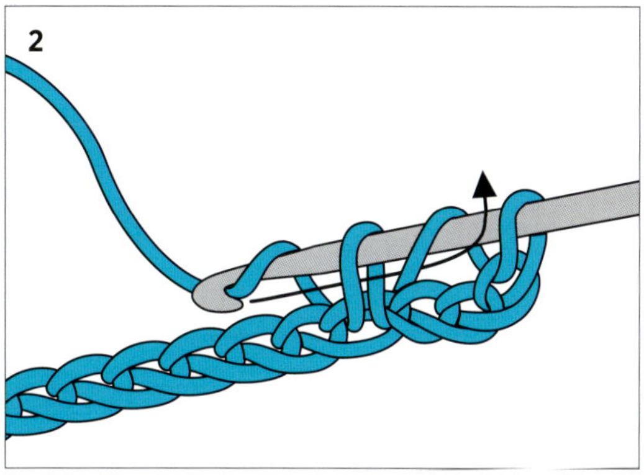

3 Yarn over again, and pull through the remaining 2 loops on the hook together (= decrease). Work all following double crochets in the next stitch (unless the instructions say otherwise).

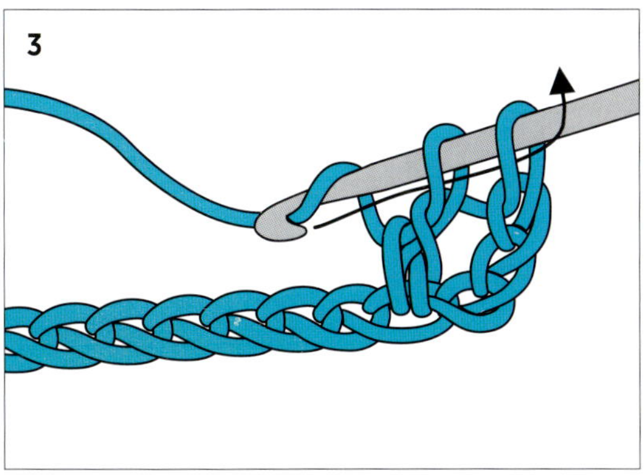

FRONT POST DOUBLE CROCHET

Yarn over. Insert the hook from the front into the gap before the post of the double crochet of the previous row. Push the hook through to the other side, yarn over, and pull the yarn back around the double crochet, pulling up a loop. Repeat 2x, pulling the yarn through 2 loops each.

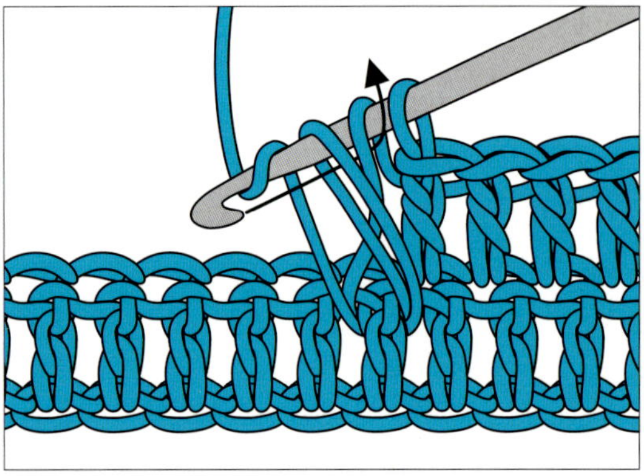

BACK POST DOUBLE CROCHET

Yarn over. Insert the hook from the back to the front around the post of the double crochet of the previous row. Push the hook to the back again. Yarn over, and finish the stitch.

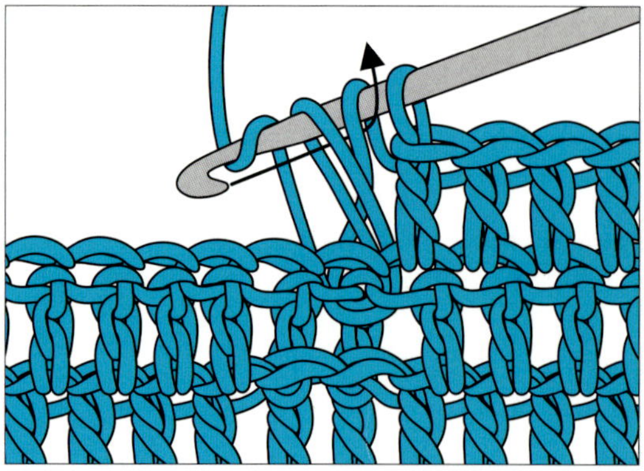

STITCHING IN THE BACK LOOP

Only insert the hook in the back, and pull the yarn through. Then work the stitch as usual.

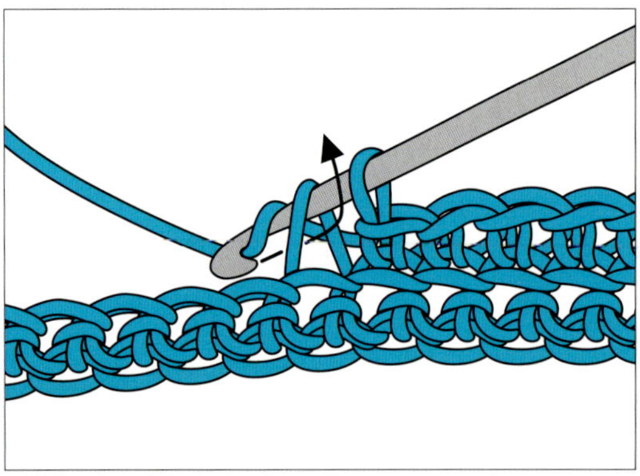

DECREASING STITCHES TOGETHER

1 Work several stitches in the same stitch or different stitches until the last step. Only perform this step for all stitches at once at the last stitch: yarn over, and pull through all the loops. (Below: Decreasing double crochets together)

2 Decreasing single crochets together.

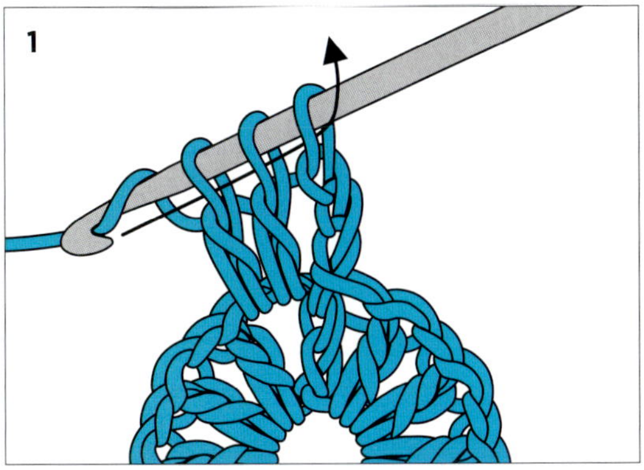

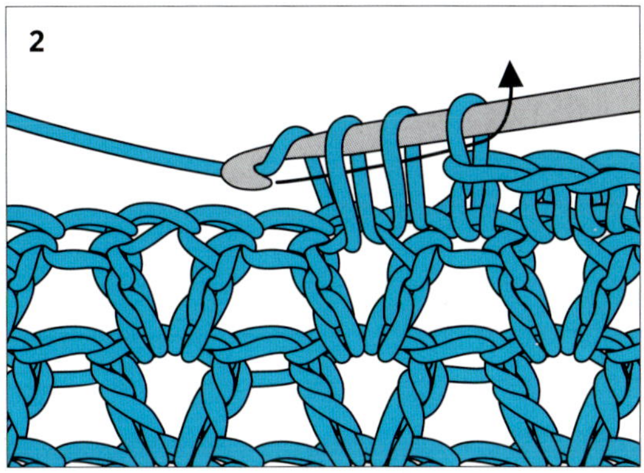

WORKING SEVERAL STITCHES IN THE SAME STITCH

Work several stitches one after the other, always inserting the hook in the same stitch—that is, the same place in the stitch from the previous row. (Below: Single crochets)

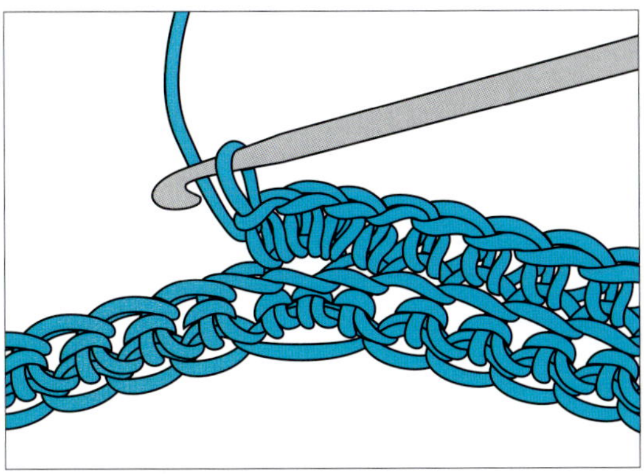

FINISHING THE WORK

Once you've reached the last stitch, cut the yarn to approx 6 in so that the tail end can be sewn up. Pull the yarn through the last stitch, and pull tight. This will form the final knot.

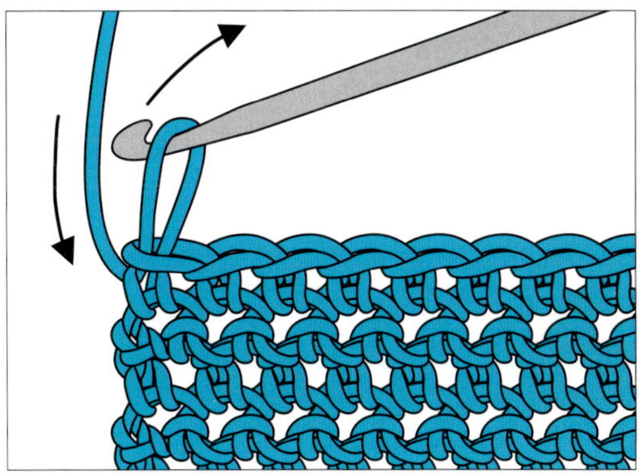

TYING ON FRINGES

1 For each fringe cut the yarns according to the instructions. Insert the hook from top to bottom in the desired stitch on the back of the work. Pick up the yarns with the hook in the center.

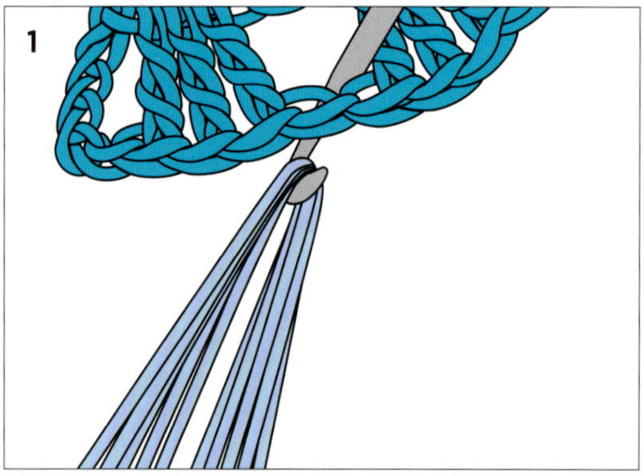

2 Pull the yarns through together to create a loop.

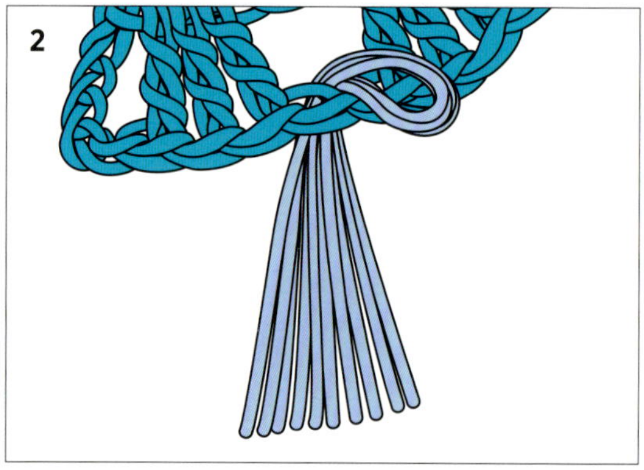

3 Insert the hook in the loop, pick up the yarns and pull through together. Pull the yarns together tightly, tying the loop to a knot. Cut back the yarns evenly.

TIP: TURNING CHAINS

At the end of a row or round, you make turning chains to move up to the next row of stitches. The number of stitches needed depends on the type of stitch and is given in the instructions. With higher stitch types, the turning chains replace the 1st stitch of the row / round: you only insert the hook in the 2nd stitch and work the last stitch in the topmost turning chain. Follow this rule of thumb:

Single crochet: 1 turning chain, insert the hook in the 1st stitch of the previous row / round.
Half double crochet: 2 turning chains, insert the hook in the 1st or 2nd stitch of the previous row / round.
Double crochet: 3 turning chains, insert the hook in the 2nd stitch of the previous row / round.
Treble crochet: 4 turning chains, insert the hook in the 2nd stitch of the previous row / round.
Double treble crochet: 5 turning chains, insert the hook in the 2nd stitch of the previous row / round.

YARN CONVERSIONS

The yarns noted here are the closest substitutes readily available to the US. For easy reference, the corresponding original yarn color is noted in parentheses after each substitution color. Please note that there may be slight variances in color, yardage, and weight, so be sure to modify your skein quantities, check your gauge, and modify the hook and pattern sizes as needed.

Austermann Baby Cotton

SUB: Hobbii Rainbow Cotton 8/4
175 yds / 1.8 oz
100% cotton
002 Natural White (10 Natural)
009 Black (02 Black)
010 Anthracite Gray (06 Taupe)
014 Silver Gray (Flecked gray 07)
078 Steel Blue (25 Fjord)
090 Egg Yolk (23 Corn yellow)
101 Rust (22 Tangerine)

Austermann Merino 120

SUB: Cascade 220 Superwash Merino
220 yds / 3.5 oz
100% superwash merino
01 Cream (110 Natural)
13 Jolly Green (173 Grass-green)
52 Blue Indigo (104 Navy)
53 Country Blue (123 Jeans blue)
58 Iguana (170 Olive)
84 Peridot (140 Absinthe)
90 Pastel Turquoise (162 Blue curaçao)
111 Freesia (175 Lemon)
114 Bluejay (132 Royal Blue)
115 Cyan Blue (133 Petrol blue)

Austermann Merino 160

SUB: Hobbii Friends Extra Fine Merino
80 yds / 1.8 oz
100% superwash merino wool
04 Cream (266 Powder)
44 Rose (256 Lollipop)
52 Dusty Rose (261 Azalea)
57 Boysenberry (241 Pink lipstick)
90 Capri Blue (235 Turquoise)
95 Dark Turquoise (233 Petrol blue)
112 Bottle Green (273 Grass-green)
113 Misty Green (259 Mint)
117 Light Gray (228 Light gray)

Buttinette Woll Butt Camilla

SUB: Scheepjes Catona
137 yd / 1.8 oz
100% mercerized cotton
74 Mercury (354.41 Gray)
106 Snow White (354.32 White)
110 Jet Black (354.35 Black)
162 Black Coffee (218.77 Chocolate)
164 Light Navy (103.768 Navy)
179 Topaz (354.36 Vanilla)
189 Royal Orange (354.43 Orange)
192 Scarlet (359.80 Bordeaux)
212 Sage Green (359.33 Green)
242 Metal Gray (271.55 Dark gray)
252 Watermelon (115.78 Lobster red)
397 Cyan (354.34 Turquoise)
404 English Tea (103.767 Beige)
505 Linen (103.769 Natural)
510 Sky Blue (240.39 Aqua)
512 Lime (354.38 Pale green)
523 Sweet Mandarin (142.56 Powder)
525 Fir (102.688 Fir)
527 Midnight (354.44 Royal Blue)

Buttinette Woll Butt Primo Madeleine

SUB: Ewe Ewe Yarns Ewe So Sporty
145 yd / 1.8 oz
100% superwash merino wool
20 Red Poppy (99.378.32 Dark red)
23 Red Velvet (99.381.47 Bordeaux)
24 Persimmon (99.103.822 Heather)
25 Orange Peel (99.381.36 Terracotta)
30 Saffron (99.240.89 Camel)
40 Lemon Chiffon (99.142.42 Multi)
50 Pistachio (102.911 Sage)
90 Vanilla (142.30 Wool white)
92 Wheat (229.93 Taupe)
97 Brushed Silver (103.823 Light gray)
98 Charcoal (253.47 Dark gray)

YARN CONVERSIONS (Cont.)

Junghans Wolle Cotton Superfine II

SUB: Scheepjes Organicon
186 yd / 1.8 oz
100% mercerized cotton
209 Desert Bloom (139-490 Salmon)
219 Oxygen (105-319 Ecru)
242 Oat Bath (139-597 Beige)
245 Amaranth (109-641)
249 Pink Petunia (105-337 Rose)
265 Morning Mist (139-599 Silver)

Junghans Wolle Recycle & PET

SUB: Berroco Remix Light
216 yd / 1.8 oz
30% nylon, 25% cotton, 24% acrylic, 10% silk, 9% linen
6959 Marmalade (142-637 Salmon)
6929 Bubblegum (142-635 Fuchsia)
6901 Birch (142-639 Wool white)
6930 Smoke (142-636 Light gray)

Lana Grossa Cool Wool Vintage

SUB: Hobbii Friends Extra Fine Merino
180 yd / 1.8 oz
100% superwash merino wool
28 Mustard (7362 Mustard)
48 Dark Magenta (7365 Plum)
73 Lavender (7372 Violet)
81 Dark Denim (7366 Dark blue)
109 Olive (7361 Olive)
119 Gray (7369 Light gray)
122 Anthracite (7370 Anthracite)

Lana Grossa Soft Cotton

SUB: Scheepjes Softfun
153 yd / 1.8 oz
60% cotton, 40% acrylic
2412 Snow (10 White)
2495 Hot Pink (14 Cyclamen)
2511 Dark Turquoise (29 Turquoise)
2612 Butterscotch (42 Curry)
2622 Latte (02 Ecru)
2644 Lagoon (48 Opal green)
2651 Pumpkin (27 Bright orange)

Langyarns Baby Cotton

SUB: Scheepjes Organicon
186 yd / 1.8 oz
100% mercerized cotton
200 Clouded Crystal (0096 Beige)
205 Lavender (00146 Violet)
209 Desert Bloom (0028 Apricot)
213 Sapling (0044 Lime)
217 Fresh Air (0178 Indigo)
245 Amaranth (0048 Pale red)
254 Steel Blue (0033 Blue)
259 Lucky Heather (0007 Lilac)
265 Morning Mist (0091 Pale green)

Langyarns Merino 120

SUB: Trendsetter Merino 6 Ply
135 yd / 1.8 oz
100% superfine merino wool
4 Bordeaux (0562 Red)
200 Black (0004 Black)
208 Sage (0098 Fir green)
335 Eggplant (0480 Bordeaux)
779 Toffee (0428 Apricot)
7800 Ecru (0001 Natural)
9067 New Leaf Green (0091 Linden green)
9509 Marine (0233 Blue)
9965 Cognac (0515 Terra cotta)
10046 Paper Sand (0226 Beige)
10083 Sunshine (0149 Yellow)
13158 Faded Jeans (0134 Pale blue)
14393 Flamingo Pink (0219 Pink)
14445 Indian Rose (0129 Raspberry)
14533 Cadet Green (0098 Petrol green)
14574 Dark Melon (0287 Dusky pink)
14608 Ocean Wave (0174 Mint)
14757 Dried Parsley (0398 Moss)
19004 Mulberry (0566 Cyclamen)

Langyarns Venus

SUB: Scheepjes Cotton Create
186 yd / 1.8 oz
50% cotton, 50% acrylic
510 Pin (0066 Red)
642 Design (0044 Lime)
652 Swatch (0040 Ice blue)
653 Fringe (0009 Pink)
661 Twist (0047 Purple)
722 Mend (0077 Terracotta)
724 Turn (0074 Petrol green)

ONline Linie 23 Club

SUB: Berroco Modern Cotton DK
335 yd / 3.5 oz
60% cotton, 40% rayon
6627 Del (12 Yellow)
6639 Waterfire (30 Raspberry)
6675 Dexter Park (21 Coral)
6692 Breakers (16 Rose)
6696 RISD (28 Salmon)
66102 Bryant (34 Vanilla)

ONline Linie 107 Supersoft

SUB: Ewe Ewe Yarns Ewe So Sporty
145 yd / 1.8 oz
100% superwash merino wool
05 Cotton Candy (264 Apricot)
25 Orange Peel (264 Coral)
40 Lemon Chiffon (246 Vanilla)
90 Vanilla (19 Natural)

ONline Linie 110 Timona

SUB: Cascade Yarns Elysian
219 yd / 3.5 oz
60% wool, 40% acrylic
01 White (23 Ecru)
18 White Swan (35 Taupe)
67 Dusty Lavender (46 Purple)

Schoeller + Stahl Limone

SUB: Scheepjes Catona
137 yd / 1.8 oz
100% mercerized cotton
106 Snow White (06 Brilliant white)
246 Icy Pink (108 Pink)
280 Lemon (100 Yellow)
108 Pink (197 Anemone)
208 Yellow Gold (192 Gold)
105 Bridal White (73 Natural)
201 Electric Blue (21 Polar blue)
392 Lime Juice (14 May green)

ABOUT THE AUTHOR

Since her teenage days, knitting and crocheting have been a part of her everyday life: **Babette Ulmer** studied fashion design, focusing on everything to do with stitches, and turned her beloved hobby into a profession. After several years of occupational experience, she turned freelance in 2001. She works for several companies in the needlecraft industry, designing patterns and writing instructions. In 2007 she became an author as well, and has since written numerous bestselling needlecraft books, including *Knitting: Step-by-Step Basics* and *How to Knit Sweaters*.

ACKNOWLEDGMENTS

Thank you to the team of crochet enthusiasts who worked the patterns shown in this book: Annette Krupka, Constanze Wisotzki, Birgit Schwer, Maria Böhly, and Babette Ulmer.

We would like to thank the following companies that kindly provided the yarns for the patterns in this book: Austermann (www.austermann.de); Buttinette (buttinette.com); Junghans Wolle (www.junghanswolle.de); Lana Grossa (www.lana-grossa.de); Langyarns (www.langyarns.com); ONline (online-garne.de); Schoeller + Stahl (schoeller-wolle.de).

weldon**owen**
an imprint of Insight Editions
P.O. Box 3088
San Rafael, CA 94912
www.weldonowen.com

CEO Raoul Goff
SVP Group Publisher Jeff McLaughlin
VP Publisher Roger Shaw
Associate Publisher Thom O'Hearn
Executive Editor Karyn Gerhard
Editorial Assistant Jon Ellis
Production Editor Ivy Long
Art Director Megan Sinead Bingham
Production Designer Jean Hwang
VP Manufacturing Alix Nicholaeff
Senior Production Manager Joshua Smith
Strategic Production Planner Lina s Palma-Temena

Weldon Owen would also like to thank BJ Berti, Meaghan Schmaltz, and Melanie McFadyen for their work on this project.

PHOTO CREDITS
Shutterstock: p11 Maya Shustov; p13 Tina Seidel; p15 kle555.

First published in Germany in 2026 by
Christian Verlag GmbH
Infanteriestrasse 11 a
80797 Munich
Germany

ISBN: 979-8-88674-389-0

Manufactured in China by Insight Editions
10 9 8 7 6 5 4 3 2 1

ROOTS of PEACE   REPLANTED PAPER

Insight Editions, in association with Roots of Peace, will plant two trees for each tree used in the manufacturing of this book. Roots of Peace is an internationally renowned humanitarian organization dedicated to eradicating land mines worldwide and converting war-torn lands into productive farms and wildlife habitats. Roots of Peace will plant two million fruit and nut trees in Afghanistan and provide farmers there with the skills and support necessary for sustainable land use.